OECD/G20 Base Erosion and Profit Shifting Project

Country-by-Country Reporting – Compilation of 2024 Peer Review Reports

INCLUSIVE FRAMEWORK ON BEPS: ACTION 13

OECD

BETTER POLICIES FOR BETTER LIVES

This document, as well as any data and map included herein, are without prejudice to the status of or sovereignty over any territory, to the delimitation of international frontiers and boundaries and to the name of any territory, city or area.

The statistical data for Israel are supplied by and under the responsibility of the relevant Israeli authorities. The use of such data by the OECD is without prejudice to the status of the Golan Heights, East Jerusalem and Israeli settlements in the West Bank under the terms of international law.

Note by the Republic of Türkiye
The information in this document with reference to "Cyprus" relates to the southern part of the Island. There is no single authority representing both Turkish and Greek Cypriot people on the Island. Türkiye recognises the Turkish Republic of Northern Cyprus (TRNC). Until a lasting and equitable solution is found within the context of the United Nations, Türkiye shall preserve its position concerning the "Cyprus issue".

Note by all the European Union Member States of the OECD and the European Union
The Republic of Cyprus is recognised by all members of the United Nations with the exception of Türkiye. The information in this document relates to the area under the effective control of the Government of the Republic of Cyprus.

Please cite this publication as:
OECD (2024), *Country-by-Country Reporting – Compilation of 2024 Peer Review Reports: Inclusive Framework on BEPS: Action 13*, OECD/G20 Base Erosion and Profit Shifting Project, OECD Publishing, Paris, https://doi.org/10.1787/f3d3f36f-en.

ISBN 978-92-64-89230-9 (print)
ISBN 978-92-64-55236-4 (PDF)
ISBN 978-92-64-39366-0 (HTML)
ISBN 978-92-64-66250-6 (epub)

OECD/G20 Base Erosion and Profit Shifting Project
ISSN 2313-2604 (print)
ISSN 2313-2612 (online)

Photo credits: Cover © ninog-Fotolia.com.

Corrigenda to OECD publications may be found at: https://www.oecd.org/en/publications/support/corrigenda.html.

Foreword

Digitalisation and globalisation have had a profound impact on economies and the lives of people around the world, and this impact has only accelerated in the 21st century. These changes have brought with them challenges to the rules for taxing international business income, which have prevailed for more than a hundred years and created opportunities for base erosion and profit shifting (BEPS), requiring bold moves by policy makers to restore confidence in the system and ensure that profits are taxed where economic activities take place and value is created.

In 2013, the OECD ramped up efforts to address these challenges in response to growing public and political concerns about tax avoidance by large multinationals. The OECD and G20 countries joined forces and developed an Action Plan to address BEPS in September 2013. The Action Plan identified 15 actions aimed at introducing coherence in the domestic rules that affect cross-border activities, reinforcing substance requirements in the existing international standards, and improving transparency as well as certainty.

After two years of work, measures in response to the 15 actions, including those published in an interim form in 2014, were consolidated into a comprehensive package and delivered to G20 Leaders in November 2015. The BEPS package represents the first substantial renovation of the international tax rules in almost a century. As the BEPS measures are implemented, it is expected that profits will be reported where the economic activities that generate them are carried out and where value is created. BEPS planning strategies that rely on outdated rules or on poorly co-ordinated domestic measures will be rendered ineffective.

OECD and G20 countries also agreed to continue to work together to ensure a consistent and co ordinated implementation of the BEPS recommendations and to make the project more inclusive. As a result, they created the OECD/G20 Inclusive Framework on BEPS (Inclusive Framework), bringing all interested and committed countries and jurisdictions on an equal footing in the Committee on Fiscal Affairs and its subsidiary bodies. With over 140 members, the Inclusive Framework monitors and peer reviews the implementation of the minimum standards and is completing the work on standard setting to address BEPS issues. In addition to its members, other international organisations and regional tax bodies are involved in the work of the Inclusive Framework, which also consults business and the civil society on its different work streams.

Although implementation of the BEPS package is dramatically changing the international tax landscape and improving the fairness of tax systems, one of the key outstanding BEPS issues – to address the tax challenges arising from the digitalisation of the economy – remained unresolved. In a major step forward on 8 October 2021, over 135 Inclusive Framework members, representing more than 95% of global GDP, joined a two-pillar solution to reform the international taxation rules and ensure that multinational enterprises pay a fair share of tax wherever they operate and generate profits in today's digitalised and globalised world economy.

This report was approved by the Inclusive Framework on 20 August 2024 and prepared for publication by the OECD Secretariat.

Table of contents

Abbreviations and acronyms

AEOI	Automatic Exchange of Information
BEPS	Base Erosion and Profit Shifting
CAA	Competent Authority Agreement
CbC	Country-by-Country
CbCR	Country-by-Country Reporting
CTS	Common Transmission System
DTC	Double Tax Convention
EOI	Exchange of Information
EU	European Union
MAAC	Convention on Mutual Administrative Assistance in Tax Matters
MCAA	Multilateral Competent Authority Agreement
MNE	Multinational Enterprise
OECD	Organisation for Economic Co-operation and Development
PE	Permanent Establishment
QCAA	Qualifying Competent Authority Agreement
SPE	Surrogate Parent Entity
TIEA	Tax Information Exchange Agreement
TP	Transfer Pricing
UPE	Ultimate Parent Entity
XML	Extensible Mark-up Language

Executive summary

Context of Country-by-Country Reporting

1. A key component of the transparency pillar of the OECD/G20 Base Erosion and Profit Shifting (BEPS) Project is the obligation for all large multinational enterprise groups (MNE Groups) with consolidated group revenue above an agreed threshold to file a Country-by-Country (CbC) report. The BEPS Action 13 Report (*Transfer Pricing Documentation and Country-by-Country Reporting*) provides a template for these MNE Groups to report annually, and for each tax jurisdiction in which they do business, the amount of revenue, profit before income tax and income tax paid and accrued, as well as the number of employees, stated capital, retained earnings and tangible assets. MNE Groups should also identify each entity within the group doing business in a particular jurisdiction and provide an indication of the business activities each entity is engaged in. As a result of BEPS Action 13, tax administrations around the world are receiving information on large foreign-headed MNE Groups which was not previously available, enabling them to better understand the structure of a group's business and enhancing their risk assessment capacity.

2. In general, the Ultimate Parent Entity (UPE) of an MNE Group will prepare and file its CbC report with the tax administration in its jurisdiction of tax residence. That tax administration will automatically exchange the CbC report with the tax administration in each jurisdiction listed in the CbC report as being a place in which the MNE Group has a Constituent Entity resident for tax purposes. This will be carried out under an International Agreement (such as the Multilateral Convention on Mutual Administrative Assistance in Tax Matters (MAAC), a Double Tax Convention (DTC) or a Tax Information Exchange Agreement (TIEA) permitting automatic exchange of information (AEOI). A Qualifying Competent Authority Agreement (QCAA) that sets out the operational details of the exchange of CbC reports will also need to be in place.

3. As one of the four BEPS minimum standards, the Country-by-Country reporting (CbCR) requirements contained in the 2015 BEPS Action 13 Report are subject to peer review in order to ensure timely and accurate implementation and thus safeguard the level playing field. All members of the Inclusive Framework on BEPS (the Inclusive Framework) commit to implementing the BEPS Action 13 minimum standard and to participating in the peer review, on an equal footing.

4. Implementation of CbC reporting is well advanced, as the peer review process evidences, with over 115 jurisdictions having now introduced an obligation for relevant MNE Groups to file a CbC report in their domestic legal framework.

Scope of this review

5. This is the seventh annual peer review for the BEPS Action 13 minimum standard. It covers 138 jurisdictions which provided legislation and/or information relating to their implementation of CbC Reporting.[1]

6. For each jurisdiction, the review covers the domestic legal and administrative framework, the exchange of information framework and measures in place to ensure the confidentiality and appropriate use of CbC reports.

Key findings

7. The key findings of the seventh annual peer review are as follows:

- ***Domestic legal and administrative framework***: Over 115 jurisdictions have a domestic legal framework for CbC reporting in place. In addition, a number of jurisdictions have final legislation approved that is awaiting official publication. In this peer review report, 19 jurisdictions have received a general recommendation to put in place or finalise their domestic legal or administrative framework and 37 jurisdictions received one or more recommendations for improvements to specific areas of their framework.
- ***Exchange of information framework:*** Of the jurisdictions included in this review, 93 jurisdictions have multilateral or bilateral competent authority agreements in place.
- ***Confidentiality:*** Of the jurisdictions included in this review, 99 have undergone an assessment by the Global Forum on Transparency and Exchange of Information for Tax Purposes (the Global Forum) concerning confidentiality and data safeguards in the context of implementing the AEOI standard, and did not receive any action plan.
- ***Appropriate use:*** 84 jurisdictions have provided detailed information, enabling the Inclusive Framework to obtain sufficient assurance that measures are in place to ensure the appropriate use of CbC reports.

8. A number of Inclusive Framework members are not included in this peer review report, either because they joined the Inclusive Framework after 1 October 2023 (at which point it was too late to incorporate them into the current peer review process) or they opted out of the peer review in accordance with the peer review terms of reference. Jurisdictions opting out of the peer review are required to confirm that they do not have any resident entities that are the UPE of an MNE Group above the consolidated group revenue threshold and that they will not require local filing of CbC reports. Members of the Inclusive Framework that are not included in this peer review report are:

- Cook Islands
- Fiji
- Kuwait
- Moldova
- Philippines
- Saint Kitts and Nevis
- Samoa

Next steps

9. The peer review of the BEPS Action 13 minimum standard is an annual process. Work will continue to monitor the implementation and operation of CbC reporting by members of the Inclusive Framework and to highlight progress made by jurisdictions to address recommendations that have been made.

Note

[1] The Russian Federation and Belarus have not been included in the peer review process for this year. A copy of the Russian Federation's peer review report for 2021 and a copy of Belarus's report for 2022 are included in this report for information.

1 The peer review of the BEPS Action 13 minimum standard on Country-by-Country Reporting

Background

11. The Country-by-Country (CbC) reporting requirements contained in the 2015 BEPS Action 13 Report (OECD, 2015[1]) form one of the four BEPS minimum standards. Each of the four BEPS minimum standards is subject to peer review in order to ensure timely and accurate implementation and thus safeguard the level playing field. All members of the Inclusive Framework commit to implementing the BEPS Action 13 minimum standard and to participating in the peer review, on an equal footing.

12. The purpose of a peer review is to ensure the effective and consistent implementation of an agreed standard and to recognise progress made by jurisdictions in this regard.

13. The peer review is a review of the legal and administrative framework put in place by a jurisdiction to implement the CbC reporting standard.

Outline of the key aspects assessed in the annual report

14. This peer review report contains the findings of the seventh annual peer review process undertaken by an Ad Hoc Joint Working Party 6 / Working Party 10 sub-group referred to as the "CbC Reporting Group". This focuses on each jurisdiction's domestic legal and administrative framework, its exchange of information network, and its measures to ensure the confidentiality and appropriate use of CbC reports.

15. The structure of each section relating to a specific reviewed jurisdiction is as follows:

- summary of filing requirements
- a table summarising any recommendations issued
- domestic legal and administrative framework
- exchange of information
- appropriate use.

16. Jurisdictions which joined the Inclusive Framework after 1 October 2023 have not been reviewed as part of this annual peer review process. These jurisdictions will be included in the next peer review process.

17. This peer review evaluates an Inclusive Framework member's implementation of the BEPS Action 13 minimum standard against an agreed set of criteria.[1] These criteria are set out in terms of reference, which include each of the elements that a jurisdiction needs to demonstrate it has fulfilled in order to show

proper implementation of the standard. These terms of reference are supplemented by additional questions for jurisdictions concerning measures they have implemented to ensure the appropriate use of CbC reporting information.

18. An agreed peer review methodology sets out the process for undertaking peer reviews of jurisdictions' compliance with the BEPS Action 13 minimum standard on Country-by-Country (CbC) reporting. This methodology sets out the scope of the peer review, the information that will be used to conduct reviews, the timelines and procedures for a review, an outline of a peer review report, the process for discussion and approval of reviews, and the confidentiality of peer review documents. A new methodology published in 2020 replaces one agreed by the Inclusive Framework in 2017, which expired with the completion of the third annual peer review in September 2020. There has been no change to the terms of reference agreed by the Inclusive Framework in 2017.

19. The Global Forum has conducted preliminary expert assessments of confidentiality and data safeguards with respect to the standard on automatic exchange of information. Given its expertise in this area, the CbC Reporting Group has relied on the work and conclusions of the Global Forum. As it contains non-public information on jurisdictions' internal systems and procedures, the outcomes of that work are not published and no further details of the review of confidentiality are provided in this compilation of peer review reports.

20. The terms of reference and methodology do not alter the BEPS Action 13 minimum standard. Any terms used in the terms of reference or methodology, and capitalised terms in this report, take their meaning from the language and context of the 2015 BEPS Action 13 Report and the references therein.

21. Jurisdictions' individual sections in this report generally reflect the status of implementation as of 31 March 2024 with the exception of information on the exchange of CbC reports which reflects the position as of 31 December 2023.

Reference

OECD (2015), *Transfer Pricing Documentation and Country-by-Country Reporting, Action 13 - 2015 Final Report*, OECD/G20 Base Erosion and Profit Shifting Project, OECD Publishing, Paris, https://doi.org/10.1787/9789264241480-en. [1]

Note

[1] https://www.oecd.org/tax/beps/beps-action-13-on-country-by-country-reporting-peer-review-documents.pdf (approved by the Inclusive Framework in October 2020.).

2 Peer review reports

Albania

Overview of CbC reporting requirements

First reporting fiscal year: Commencing on or after 1 January 2024

Consolidated group revenue threshold: ALL 105 billion

Filing deadline: 12 months following the end of the reporting fiscal year

Local filing required: No

Surrogate parent entity filing permitted: No

First review of the domestic legal framework: 2023/2024

Summary of recommendations

Area of implementation	Recommendations for improvement
Domestic legal and administrative framework	None.
Exchange of information framework	It is recommended that Albania take steps to implement the necessary processes or written procedures to ensure that the exchange of information is conducted in a manner consistent with the terms of reference relating to the exchange of information framework.
Appropriate use	None.

The domestic legal and administrative framework

Albania has now introduced a CbC reporting filing requirement which applies to all Ultimate Parent Entities of MNE Groups above a certain threshold and which requires inclusion of all constituent entities.[1]

A CbC reporting filing obligation applies in Albania for fiscal years commencing on or after 1 January 2024 and filing is required 12 months after the reporting year end. Albania has enforcement requirements to ensure compliance with rules on CbC reporting.

Albania's domestic legal and administrative framework meets all terms of reference.

The exchange of information framework

Albania has qualifying competent authority agreements in effect with jurisdictions of the Inclusive Framework that meet the confidentiality, consistency and appropriate use conditions and with which Albania has an international exchange of information agreement in effect that allows for the automatic exchange of tax information. Albania has activated relationships under the Multilateral Competent Authority Agreement for exchanging CbC reports.

It is recommended that Albania take steps to implement the necessary processes or written procedures to ensure that the exchange of information is conducted in a manner consistent with the terms of reference relating to the exchange of information framework.

Appropriate use of CbC reports

Albania has provided information that confirms that it has controls in place to ensure the appropriate use of CbC reports.

Albania meets all terms of reference with respect to the appropriate use condition.

Note

[1] https://www.tatime.gov.al/c/6/69/procedurat-tatimore.

Andorra

Overview of CbC reporting requirements

First reporting fiscal year: Commencing on or after 1 January 2018

Consolidated group revenue threshold: EUR 750 million

Filing deadline: 12 months following the end of the reporting fiscal year

Local filing required: Yes

Surrogate parent entity filing permitted: Yes

First review of the domestic legal framework: 2017/2018

Summary of recommendations

Area of implementation	Recommendations for improvement
Domestic legal and administrative framework	None.
Exchange of information framework	None.
Appropriate use	None.

The domestic legal and administrative framework

Andorra confirms that its rules have not changed and continue to be applied effectively. Andorra continues to meet all terms of reference.

The exchange of information framework

Andorra confirms that its rules have not changed and continue to be applied effectively. Andorra continues to meet all terms of reference.

Appropriate use of CbC reports

Andorra confirms that its rules have not changed and continue to be applied effectively. Andorra continues to meet all terms of reference.

Angola

Overview of CbC reporting requirements

Angola has not yet introduced a requirement for the filing of CbC reports, as required under the BEPS Action 13 (CbC reporting) minimum standard.

Summary of recommendations

Area of implementation	Recommendations for improvement
Domestic legal and administrative framework	It is recommended that Angola take steps to implement a domestic legal and administrative framework to impose and enforce CbC reporting requirements as soon as possible.
Exchange of information framework	It is recommended that Angola take steps to have qualifying competent authority agreements in effect with jurisdictions of the Inclusive Framework that meet the confidentiality, consistency and appropriate use conditions and with which Angola has an international exchange of information agreement in effect that allows for the automatic exchange of tax information. It is recommended that Angola take steps to implement the necessary processes or written procedures to ensure that the exchange of information is conducted in a manner consistent with the terms of reference relating to the exchange of information framework.
Appropriate use	It is recommended that Angola take steps to ensure that the appropriate use condition is met ahead of the first exchanges of information.

The domestic legal and administrative framework

Angola does not yet have legislation in place to implement the BEPS Action 13 minimum standard.

It is recommended that Angola take steps to implement a domestic legal and administrative framework to impose and enforce CbC reporting requirements as soon as possible. This recommendation remains in place since the 2017/2018 peer review.

The exchange of information framework

Angola has no bilateral relationships in place for the exchange of CbC reports nor processes to ensure that the exchange of information is conducted in a manner consistent with the terms of reference relating to the exchange of information framework.

It is recommended that Angola take steps to have qualifying competent authority agreements in effect with jurisdictions of the Inclusive Framework that meet the confidentiality, consistency and appropriate use conditions and with which Angola has an international exchange of information agreement in effect that allows for the automatic exchange of tax information. This recommendation remains in place since the 2017/2018 peer review.

It is recommended that Angola take steps to implement the necessary processes or written procedures to ensure that the exchange of information is conducted in a manner consistent with the terms of reference relating to the exchange of information framework. This recommendation remains in place since the 2018/2019 peer review.

Appropriate use of CbC reports

Angola does not yet have controls in place to ensure the appropriate use of CbC reports.

It is recommended that Angola take steps to ensure that the appropriate use condition is met ahead of the first exchanges of information. This recommendation remains in place since the 2017/2018 peer review.

Anguilla

Overview of CbC reporting requirements

First reporting fiscal year: Commencing on or after 1 January 2019

Consolidated group revenue threshold: USD 850 million

Filing deadline: 12 months following the end of the reporting fiscal year

Local filing required: No

Surrogate parent entity filing permitted: Yes

First review of the domestic legal framework: 2018/2019

Summary of recommendations

Area of implementation	Recommendations for improvement
Domestic legal and administrative framework	None.
Exchange of information framework	None.
Appropriate use	Not reviewed.

The domestic legal and administrative framework

Anguilla confirms that its rules have not changed and continue to be applied effectively. Anguilla continues to meet all terms of reference.

The exchange of information framework

Anguilla's confirms that its rules have not changed and continue to be applied effectively. Anguilla continues to meet all terms of reference.

Appropriate use of CbC reports

Anguilla is a non-reciprocal jurisdiction and, as such, will not receive CbC reports submitted to tax authorities in other jurisdictions, and will not apply local filing. It is therefore not necessary for this peer review evaluation to reach any conclusions with respect to Anguilla's compliance with the terms of reference on appropriate use.

Antigua and Barbuda

Overview of CbC reporting requirements

Antigua and Barbuda has not yet introduced a requirement for the filing of CbC reports, as required under the BEPS Action 13 (CbC reporting) minimum standard.

Summary of recommendations

Area of implementation	Recommendations for improvement
Domestic legal and administrative framework	It is recommended that Antigua and Barbuda take steps to implement a domestic legal and administrative framework to impose and enforce CbC reporting requirements as soon as possible.
Exchange of information framework	It is recommended that Antigua and Barbuda take steps to have qualifying competent authority agreements in effect with jurisdictions of the Inclusive Framework that meet the confidentiality, consistency and appropriate use conditions and with which Antigua and Barbuda has an international exchange of information agreement in effect that allows for the automatic exchange of tax information. It is recommended that Antigua and Barbuda take steps to implement the necessary processes or written procedures to ensure that the exchange of information is conducted in a manner consistent with the terms of reference relating to the exchange of information framework.
Appropriate use	It is recommended that Antigua and Barbuda take steps to ensure that the appropriate use condition is met ahead of the first exchanges of information.

The domestic legal and administrative framework

Antigua and Barbuda does not yet have legislation in place to implement the BEPS Action 13 minimum standard.

It is recommended that Antigua and Barbuda take steps to implement a domestic legal and administrative framework to impose and enforce CbC reporting requirements as soon as possible. This recommendation remains in place since the 2019/2020 peer review.

The exchange of information framework

Antigua and Barbuda has no bilateral relationships in place for the exchange of CbC reports nor processes to ensure that the exchange of information is conducted in a manner consistent with the terms of reference relating to the exchange of information framework.

It is recommended that Antigua and Barbuda take steps to have qualifying competent authority agreements in effect with jurisdictions of the Inclusive Framework that meet the confidentiality, consistency and appropriate use conditions and with which Antigua and Barbuda has an international exchange of information agreement in effect that allows for the automatic exchange of tax information. This recommendation remains in place since the 2019/2020 peer review.

It is recommended that Antigua and Barbuda take steps to implement the necessary processes or written procedures to ensure that the exchange of information is conducted in a manner consistent with the terms

of reference relating to the exchange of information framework. This recommendation remains in place since the 2019/2020 peer review.

Appropriate use of CbC reports

Antigua and Barbuda does not yet have controls in place to ensure the appropriate use of CbC reports.

It is recommended that Antigua and Barbuda take steps to ensure that the appropriate use condition is met ahead of the first exchanges of information. This recommendation remains in place since the 2019/2020 peer review.

Argentina

Overview of CbC reporting requirements

First reporting fiscal year: Commencing on or after 1 January 2017

Consolidated group revenue threshold: EUR 750 million

Filing deadline: 12 months following the end of the reporting fiscal year

Local filing required: Yes

Surrogate parent entity filing permitted: Yes

First review of the domestic legal framework: 2017/2018

Summary of recommendations

Area of implementation	Recommendations for improvement
Domestic legal and administrative framework	None.
Exchange of information framework	None.
Appropriate use	None.

The domestic legal and administrative framework

Argentina confirms that its rules have not changed and continue to be applied effectively. Argentina continues to meet all terms of reference.

The exchange of information framework

Argentina confirms that its rules have not changed and continue to be applied effectively. Argentina continues to meet all terms of reference.

Appropriate use of CbC reports

Argentina confirms that its rules have not changed and continue to be applied effectively. Argentina continues to meet all terms of reference.

Armenia

Overview of CbC reporting requirements

First reporting fiscal year: Commencing on or after 1 January 2025

Consolidated group revenue threshold: EUR 750 million

Filing deadline: 12 months following the end of the reporting fiscal year

Local filing required: No

Surrogate parent entity filing permitted: No

First review of the domestic legal framework: 2023/2024.

Summary of recommendations

Area of implementation	Recommendations for improvement
Domestic legal and administrative framework	None.
Exchange of information framework	It is recommended that Armenia take steps to have qualifying competent authority agreements in effect with jurisdictions of the Inclusive Framework that meet the confidentiality, consistency and appropriate use conditions and with which Armenia has an international exchange of information agreement in effect that allows for the automatic exchange of tax information.
Appropriate use	None.

The domestic legal and administrative framework

Armenia has introduced a CbC reporting filing requirement which applies to all Ultimate Parent Entities of MNE Groups above certain threshold, and which requires inclusion of all constituent entities.[1]

A CbC reporting filing obligation applies in Armenia for fiscal years commencing on or after 1 January 2025 and filing is required 12 months after the reporting year end.

Armenia has enforcement requirements to ensure compliance with rules on CbC reporting.

Armenia's domestic legal and administrative framework meets all terms of reference.

The exchange of information framework

Armenia has no bilateral relationships in place for the exchange of CbC reports nor processes to ensure that the exchange of information is conducted in a manner consistent with the terms of reference relating to the exchange of information framework.

It is recommended that Armenia take steps to have qualifying competent authority agreements in effect with jurisdictions of the Inclusive Framework that meet the confidentiality, consistency and appropriate use conditions and with which Armenia has an international exchange of information agreement in effect that allows for the automatic exchange of tax information. This recommendation remains in place since the 2019/2020 peer review.

Armenia's 2019/2020 peer review included a recommendation Armenia take steps to implement the necessary processes or written procedures to ensure that the exchange of information is conducted in a manner consistent with the terms of reference relating to the exchange of information framework. These processes are in place and the recommendation is now removed.

Appropriate use of CbC reports

Armenia's 2019/2020 peer review included a recommendation that Armenia take steps to ensure that the appropriate use condition is met ahead of the first exchanges of information. Armenia now has controls in place to ensure the appropriate use of CbC reports and this recommendation is removed.

Armenia meets all terms of reference with respect to the appropriate use condition.

Note

[1] https://www.src.am/storage/menu_contents_227/hr_hhpekn_2023_720l.pdf_64ba794beb212.pdf

Aruba

Overview of CbC reporting requirements

First reporting fiscal year: Commencing on or after 1 January 2019

Consolidated group revenue threshold: AWG 1.5 billion

Filing deadline: 12 months following the end of the reporting fiscal year

Local filing required: Yes

Surrogate parent entity filing permitted: Yes

First review of the domestic legal framework: 2020/2021

Summary of recommendations

Area of implementation	Recommendations for improvement
Domestic legal and administrative framework	None.
Exchange of information framework	None.
Appropriate use	None.

The domestic legal and administrative framework

Aruba has reintroduced its local filing requirement.[1]

Aruba confirms that its rules have not changed and continue to be applied effectively. Aruba continues to meet all terms of reference.

The exchange of information framework

Aruba confirms that its rules have not changed and continue to be applied effectively. Aruba continues to meet all terms of reference.

Appropriate use of CbC reports

Aruba's 2022/2023 peer report did not reach any conclusions with regard to appropriate use of CbC reports as Aruba was a non-reciprocal jurisdiction. Aruba has now notified as a reciprocal jurisdiction.

Aruba has provided details of the controls it has in place to ensure the appropriate use of CbC reports, which comply with published Guidance on the Appropriate Use of Information Contained in CbC Reports.

Aruba meets all terms of reference with respect to the appropriate use condition.

Note

[1] https://www.impuesto.aw/cbc-English-version?origin=/cbc-English%20version.

Australia

Overview of CbC reporting requirements

First reporting fiscal year: Commencing on or after 1 January 2016

Consolidated group revenue threshold: AUD 1 billion

Filing deadline: 12 months following the end of the reporting fiscal year

Local filing required: Yes

Surrogate parent entity filing permitted: Yes

First review of the domestic legal framework: 2017/2018

Summary of recommendations

Area of implementation	Recommendations for improvement
Domestic legal and administrative framework	None.
Exchange of information framework	None.
Appropriate use	None.

The domestic legal and administrative framework

Australia confirms that its rules have not changed and continue to be applied effectively. Australia continues to meet all terms of reference.

The exchange of information framework

Australia confirms that its rules have not changed and continue to be applied effectively. Australia continues to meet all terms of reference.

Appropriate use of CbC reports

Australia confirms that its rules have not changed and continue to be applied effectively. Australia continues to meet all terms of reference.

Austria

Overview of CbC reporting requirements

First reporting fiscal year: Commencing on or after 1 January 2016

Consolidated group revenue threshold: EUR 750 million

Filing deadline: 12 months following the end of the reporting fiscal year

Local filing required: Yes, for reporting fiscal years commencing on or after 1 January 2017

Surrogate parent entity filing permitted: Yes

First review of the domestic legal framework: 2017/2018

Summary of recommendations

Area of implementation	Recommendations for improvement
Domestic legal and administrative framework	None.
Exchange of information framework	None.
Appropriate use	None.

The domestic legal and administrative framework

Austria confirms that its rules have not changed and continue to be applied effectively. Austria continues to meet all terms of reference.

The exchange of information framework

Austria confirms that its rules have not changed and continue to be applied effectively. Austria continues to meet all terms of reference.

Appropriate use of CbC reports

Austria confirms that its rules have not changed and continue to be applied effectively. Austria continues to meet all terms of reference.

Azerbaijan

Overview of CbC reporting requirements

First reporting fiscal year: Commencing on or after 1 January 2020

Consolidated group revenue threshold: EUR 750 million

Filing deadline: 12 months following the end of the reporting fiscal year

Local filing required: Yes

Surrogate parent entity filing permitted: Yes

First review of the domestic legal framework: 2022/2023

Summary of recommendations

Area of implementation	Recommendations for improvement
Domestic legal and administrative framework	None.
Exchange of information framework	None.
Appropriate use	None.

The domestic legal and administrative framework

Azerbaijan confirms that its rules have not changed and continue to be applied effectively. Azerbaijan continues to meet all terms of reference.

The exchange of information framework

Azerbaijan confirms that its rules have not changed and continue to be applied effectively. Azerbaijan continues to meet all terms of reference.

Appropriate use of CbC reports

Azerbaijan confirms that its rules have not changed and continue to be applied effectively. Azerbaijan continues to meet all terms of reference.

Bahamas

Overview of CbC reporting requirements

First reporting fiscal year: Commencing on or after 1 January 2018

Consolidated group revenue threshold: USD 850 million

Filing deadline: 12 months following the end of the reporting fiscal year

Local filing required: No

Surrogate parent entity filing permitted: Yes

First review of the domestic legal framework: 2018/2019

Summary of recommendations

Area of implementation	Recommendations for improvement
Domestic legal and administrative framework	None.
Exchange of information framework	None.
Appropriate use	Not reviewed.

The domestic legal and administrative framework

The Bahamas confirms that its rules have not changed and continue to be applied effectively. The Bahamas continues to meet all terms of reference.[1]

The exchange of information framework

The Bahamas confirms that its rules have not changed and continue to be applied effectively. The Bahamas continues to meet all terms of reference.

Appropriate use of CbC reports

The Bahamas is a non-reciprocal jurisdiction and, as such, will not receive CbC reports submitted to tax authorities in other jurisdictions, and will not apply local filing. It is therefore not necessary for this peer review evaluation to reach any conclusions with respect to compliance with the terms of reference on appropriate use.

Note

[1] The Bahamas' 2018/2019 peer review included a monitoring point which remains in place. It was noted that the Bahamas' legislation includes provisions relating to (i) the deactivation of local filing in case of surrogate filing (see Section 3(4) of The Bahamas CbC Act) and (ii) the fact that a single Constituent Entity could file a CbC report that satisfies the filing requirement of all Constituent Entities of such MNE Group that are resident in the Bahamas (see Section 3(3) of The Bahamas CbC Act). While these provisions do not seem to create a filing obligation on Constituent Entities in the Bahamas (being noted that according to Section 3(1) and 3(2), only Ultimate Parent Entities and Surrogate Parent Entities shall file a CbC report in the Bahamas), they may introduce uncertainty for taxpayers. This will be monitored to ensure that no local filing obligations arise from Section 3 of the act.

Bahrain

Overview of CbC reporting requirements

First reporting fiscal year: Commencing on or after 1 January 2021

Consolidated group revenue threshold: BHD 342 million

Filing deadline: 12 months following the end of the reporting fiscal year

Local filing required: No

Surrogate parent entity filing permitted: No

First review of the domestic legal framework: 2020/2021

Summary of recommendations

Area of implementation	Recommendations for improvement
Domestic legal and administrative framework	None.
Exchange of information framework	None.
Appropriate use	Not reviewed.

The domestic legal and administrative framework

Bahrain confirms that its rules have not changed and continue to be applied effectively. Bahrain continues to meet all terms of reference.

The exchange of information framework

Bahrain confirms that its rules have not changed and continue to be applied effectively. Bahrain continues to meet all terms of reference.

Appropriate use of CbC reports

Bahrain is a non-reciprocal jurisdiction and, as such, will not receive CbC reports submitted to tax authorities in other jurisdictions, and will not apply local filing. It is therefore not necessary for this peer review evaluation to reach any conclusions with respect to compliance with the terms of reference on appropriate use.

Barbados

Overview of CbC reporting requirements

First reporting fiscal year: Commencing on or after 1 January 2021

Consolidated group revenue threshold: USD 850 million

Filing deadline: 12 months following the end of the reporting fiscal year

Local filing required: Yes

Surrogate parent entity filing permitted: Yes

First review of the domestic legal framework: 2021/2022

Summary of recommendations

Area of implementation	Recommendations for improvement
Domestic legal and administrative framework	None.
Exchange of information framework	None.
Appropriate use	None.

The domestic legal and administrative framework

Barbados confirms that its rules have not changed and continue to be applied effectively. Barbados continues to meet all terms of reference.

The exchange of information framework

Barbados confirms that its rules have not changed and continue to be applied effectively. Barbados continues to meet all terms of reference.

Appropriate use of CbC reports

Barbados confirms that its rules have not changed and continue to be applied effectively. Barbados continues to meet all terms of reference.

Belarus

Overview of CbC reporting requirements

Belarus has not yet introduced a requirement for the filing of CbC reports, as required under the BEPS Action 13 (CbC reporting) minimum standard.

Summary of recommendations

Area of implementation	Recommendations for improvement
Domestic legal and administrative framework	It is recommended that Belarus take steps to implement a domestic legal and administrative framework to impose and enforce CbC reporting requirements as soon as possible.
Exchange of information framework	It is recommended that Belarus take steps to have qualifying competent authority agreements in effect with jurisdictions of the Inclusive Framework that meet the confidentiality, consistency and appropriate use conditions and with which Belarus has an international exchange of information agreement in effect that allows for the automatic exchange of tax information. It is recommended that Belarus take steps to implement the necessary processes or written procedures to ensure that the exchange of information is conducted in a manner consistent with the terms of reference relating to the exchange of information framework.
Appropriate use	It is recommended that Belarus take steps to ensure that the appropriate use condition is met ahead of the first exchanges of information.

The domestic legal and administrative framework

Belarus does not yet have legislation in place to implement the BEPS Action 13 minimum standard.

It is recommended that Belarus take steps to implement a domestic legal and administrative framework to impose and enforce CbC reporting requirements as soon as possible.

The exchange of information framework

Belarus has no bilateral relationships in place for the exchange of CbC reports nor processes to ensure that the exchange of information is conducted in a manner consistent with the terms of reference relating to the exchange of information framework.

It is recommended that Belarus take steps to have qualifying competent authority agreements in effect with jurisdictions of the Inclusive Framework that meet the confidentiality, consistency and appropriate use conditions and with which Belarus has an international exchange of information agreement in effect that allows for the automatic exchange of tax information.

It is recommended that Belarus take steps to implement the necessary processes or written procedures to ensure that the exchange of information is conducted in a manner consistent with the terms of reference relating to the exchange of information framework.

Appropriate use of CbC reports

Belarus does not yet have controls in place to ensure the appropriate use of CbC reports.

It is recommended that Belarus take steps to ensure that the appropriate use condition is met ahead of the first exchanges of information.

Belgium

Overview of CbC reporting requirements

First reporting fiscal year: Commencing on or after 1 January 2016

Consolidated group revenue threshold: EUR 750 million

Filing deadline: 12 months following the end of the reporting fiscal year

Local filing required: Yes

Surrogate parent entity filing permitted: Yes

First review of the domestic legal framework: 2017/2018

Summary of recommendations

Area of implementation	Recommendations for improvement
Domestic legal and administrative framework	None.
Exchange of information framework	None.
Appropriate use	None.

The domestic legal and administrative framework

Belgium confirms that its rules have not changed and continue to be applied effectively. Belgium continues to meet all terms of reference.[1]

The exchange of information framework

Belgium confirms that its rules have not changed and continue to be applied effectively. Belgium continues to meet all terms of reference.

Appropriate use of CbC reports

Belgium confirms that its rules have not changed and continue to be applied effectively. Belgium continues to meet all terms of reference.

Note

[1] Belgium's 2017/2018 review included a monitoring point relating to the rule according to which where there are more than one Constituent Entities of the same MNE Group that are resident for tax purposes in

the EU, the MNE Group may designate one of such Constituent Entities to file the country-by-country report conforming to the requirements that would satisfy the filing requirement of all the Constituent Entities of such MNE Group that are resident for tax purposes in the EU. This monitoring point remains in place.

Belize

Overview of CbC reporting requirements

First reporting fiscal year: Commencing on or after 1 January 2019

Consolidated group revenue threshold: USD 850 million

Filing deadline: 12 months following the end of the reporting fiscal year

Local filing required: Requirement suspended

Surrogate parent entity filing permitted: Yes

First review of the domestic legal framework: 2019/2020

Summary of recommendations

Area of implementation	Recommendations for improvement
Domestic legal and administrative framework	None.
Exchange of information framework	None.
Appropriate use	Not reviewed.

The domestic legal and administrative framework

Belize confirms that its rules have not changed and continue to be applied effectively. Belize continues to meet all terms of reference.

The exchange of information framework

Belize confirms that its rules have not changed and continue to be applied effectively. Belize continues to meet all terms of reference.

Appropriate use of CbC reports

Belize is a non-reciprocal jurisdiction and, as such, will not receive CbC reports submitted to tax authorities in other jurisdictions, and will not apply local filing. It is not necessary for this peer review evaluation to reach any conclusion with respect to Belize's compliance with the terms of reference on appropriate use.

For information, Belize has provided details of the controls it has in place to ensure the appropriate use of CbC reports, which comply with published Guidance on the Appropriate Use of Information Contained in CbC Reports.

Benin

Overview of CbC reporting requirements

First reporting fiscal year: Commencing on or after 1 January 2020

Consolidated group revenue threshold: XOF 492 billion

Filing deadline: 12 months following the end of the reporting fiscal year

Local filing required: Yes

Surrogate parent entity filing permitted: Yes

First review of the domestic legal framework: 2022/2023

Summary of recommendations

Area of implementation	Recommendations for improvement
Domestic legal and administrative framework	It is recommended that Benin introduce or complete the definitions of a "Group", "MNE Group", "Constituent Entity", "Consolidated Financial Statements", "Fiscal Year", "Reporting Fiscal Year", "Reporting Entity", and "Systemic Failure" in a manner that is consistent with the terms of reference.
	It is recommended that Benin publish the full content and format requirements of the CbC Report.
	It is recommended that Benin take steps to ensure that local filing only occurs in the circumstances permitted under the minimum standard.
	It is recommended that Benin take steps to amend its legislation or otherwise impose a limitation on local filing in case of surrogate filing in line with the Action 13 minimum standard.
	It is recommended that Benin clarify that the annual consolidated group revenue threshold calculation rule applies in line with the OECD guidance on currency fluctuations in respect of an MNE Group whose Ultimate Parent Entity is located in a jurisdiction other than Benin.
	It is recommended that Benin take steps to ensure that enforcement provisions and monitoring relating to the enforcement of CbCR filing obligations are implemented.
Exchange of information framework	It is recommended that Benin take steps to have qualifying competent authority agreements in effect with jurisdictions of the Inclusive Framework that meet the confidentiality, consistency and appropriate use conditions and with which Benin has an international exchange of information agreement in effect that allows for the automatic exchange of tax information.
	It is recommended that Benin take steps to implement the necessary processes or written procedures to ensure that the exchange of information is conducted in a manner consistent with the terms of reference relating to the exchange of information framework.
Appropriate use	It is recommended that Benin take steps to ensure that the appropriate use condition is met ahead of the first exchanges of information.

The domestic legal and administrative framework

Benin has a number of recommendations to improve the legislation. These recommendations remain in place since the 2022/2023 peer review.

The definition of Group

Benin's legislation does not include a definition of "Group". It is recommended that Benin amend its legislation to include a definition of "Group" that is in line with the standard.

The definition of MNE Group

Benin's legislation does not include a definition of "MNE Group". It is recommended that Benin amend its legislation to include a definition of "MNE Group" that is in line with the standard.

The definition of Constituent Entity

Benin's legislation does not include a definition of "Constituent Entity". It is recommended that Benin amend its legislation to include a definition of "Constituent Entity" that is in line with the standard.

The definition of Consolidated Financial Statements

Benin's legislation does not include a definition of "Consolidated Financial Statements". It is recommended that Benin amend its legislation to include a definition of "Consolidated Financial Statements" that is in line with the standard.

The definition of Fiscal Year

Benin's legislation does not include a definition of "Fiscal Year". It is recommended that Benin amend its legislation to include a definition of "Fiscal Year" that is in line with the standard.

The definition of Reporting Fiscal Year

Benin's legislation does not include a definition of "Reporting Fiscal Year". It is recommended that Benin amend its legislation to include a definition of "Reporting Fiscal Year" that is in line with the standard.

The definition of Reporting Entity

Benin's legislation does not include a definition of "Reporting Entity". It is recommended that Benin amend its legislation to include a definition of "Reporting Entity" that is in line with the standard.

The definition of Systemic Failure

Benin's legislation does not include a definition of "Systemic Failure". It is recommended that Benin amend its legislation to include a definition of "Systemic Failure" that is in line with the standard.

Contents of the Country-by-Country report

The information included in Benin's regulation does not include the template of the Country-by-Country report and does not any details of what should be included under each heading in the report. It is recommended that Benin publish the full content and format requirements of the CbC Report.

The local filing provision

Benin has a legislative requirement for local filing which is in effect despite Benin not yet meeting all of the consistency, confidentiality and appropriate use conditions. It is therefore recommended that Benin take steps to ensure that local filing only occurs in the circumstances permitted under the minimum standard.

Limitation on local filing in case of surrogate filing

Benin's legislation does not limit local filing in case of surrogate filing. It is recommended that Benin take steps to amend its legislation or otherwise impose a limitation on local filing in case of surrogate filing in line with the minimum standard.

Currency fluctuations

Where an MNE Group draws up, or would draw up, its Consolidated Financial Statements in a currency other than that specified by Benin, the reference to Benin's threshold has the effect as if it were a reference to the equivalent in that currency at the average exchange rate for the accounting period. While this provision would not create an issue for MNE Groups whose Ultimate Parent Entity is a tax resident in Benin, it may be incompatible with the guidance on currency fluctuations for MNE Groups whose Ultimate Parent Entity is located in another jurisdiction, if local filing requirements were applied in respect of a Constituent Entity (which is a Benin tax resident) of an MNE Group which does not reach the threshold as determined in the jurisdiction of the Ultimate Parent Entity of such a Group. It is recommended that Benin clarify that the annual consolidated group revenue threshold calculation rule applies in line with the OECD guidance on currency fluctuations in respect of an MNE Group whose Ultimate Parent Entity is located in a jurisdiction other than Benin.

Effective implementation

Benin has a notification mechanism in place that apply to taxpayers in Benin. There are however no penalties or enforcement measures for failure to file and late filing and it is not clear whether penalties in relation to incorrect or incomplete filing of returns would also apply to a CbC report. It is recommended that Benin take steps to ensure that enforcement provisions and monitoring relating to the enforcement of CbCR filing obligations are implemented.

The exchange of information framework

Benin has no bilateral relationships in place for the exchange of CbC reports nor processes to ensure that the exchange of information is conducted in a manner consistent with the terms of reference relating to the exchange of information framework.

It is recommended that Benin take steps to have qualifying competent authority agreements in effect with jurisdictions of the Inclusive Framework that meet the confidentiality, consistency and appropriate use conditions and with which Benin has an international exchange of information agreement in effect that allows for the automatic exchange of tax information. This recommendation remains in place since the 2017/2018 peer review.

It is recommended that Benin take steps to implement the necessary processes or written procedures to ensure that the exchange of information is conducted in a manner consistent with the terms of reference relating to the exchange of information framework. This recommendation remains in place since the 2018/2019 peer review.

Appropriate use of CbC reports

Benin does not yet have controls in place to ensure the appropriate use of CbC reports.

It is recommended that Benin take steps to ensure that the appropriate use condition is met ahead of the first exchanges of information. This recommendation remains in place since the 2017/2018 peer review.

Bermuda

Overview of CbC reporting requirements

First reporting fiscal year: Commencing on or after 1 January 2016

Consolidated group revenue threshold: EUR 750 million

Filing deadline: 12 months following the end of the reporting fiscal year

Local filing required: No

Surrogate parent entity filing permitted: Yes

First review of the domestic legal framework: 2017/2018

Summary of recommendations

Area of implementation	Recommendations for improvement
Domestic legal and administrative framework	None.
Exchange of information framework	None.
Appropriate use	Not reviewed.

The domestic legal and administrative framework

Bermuda confirms that its rules have not changed and continue to be applied effectively. Bermuda continues to meet all terms of reference.

The exchange of information framework

Bermuda confirms that its rules have not changed and continue to be applied effectively. Bermuda continues to meet all terms of reference.

Appropriate use of CbC reports

Bermuda is a non-reciprocal jurisdiction and, as such, will not receive CbC reports submitted to tax authorities in other jurisdictions, and will not apply local filing. It is therefore not necessary for this peer review evaluation to reach any conclusions with respect to Bermuda's compliance with the terms of reference on appropriate use.

For information, Bermuda has provided details of the controls it has in place to ensure the appropriate use of CbC reports, which comply with published Guidance on the Appropriate Use of Information Contained in CbC Reports.

Bosnia and Herzegovina

Overview of CbC reporting requirements

First reporting fiscal year: Commencing on or after 1 January 2018

Consolidated group revenue threshold: BAM 1.5 billion / EUR 750 million

Filing deadline: 31 March of year following reporting year

Local filing required: No

Surrogate parent entity filing permitted: Yes

First review of the domestic legal framework: 2019/2020

Summary of recommendations

Area of implementation	Recommendations for improvement
Domestic legal and administrative framework	It is recommended that Bosnia and Herzegovina take steps to ensure that the filing requirement for CbC reporting applies equally to all relevant entities with no exemptions. It is recommended that Bosnia and Herzegovina take steps to amend legislation or otherwise clarify that the threshold requirement applies in line with the standard. It is recommended that Bosnia and Herzegovina take steps to amend legislation or otherwise ensure that the filing deadline is not more than 12 months from the end of the reporting fiscal year. It is recommended that Bosnia and Herzegovina take steps to implement procedures to ensure compliance with its filing requirement.
Exchange of information framework	It is recommended that Bosnia and Herzegovina take steps to have qualifying competent authority agreements in effect with jurisdictions of the Inclusive Framework which meet the confidentiality, consistency and appropriate use conditions and with which Bosnia and Herzegovina has an international exchange of information agreement in effect that allows for the automatic exchange of tax information. It is recommended that Bosnia and Herzegovina take steps to implement the necessary processes or written procedures to ensure that the exchange of information is conducted in a manner consistent with the terms of reference relating to the exchange of information framework.
Appropriate use	It is recommended that Bosnia and Herzegovina take steps to ensure that the appropriate use condition is met ahead of the first exchanges of information.

The domestic legal and administrative framework

Bosnia and Herzegovina has filing requirements which apply inconsistently and which are not in line with the standard.

It is recommended that Bosnia and Herzegovina take steps to ensure that the filing requirement for CbC applies equally to all relevant entities with no exemptions.

It is recommended that Bosnia and Herzegovina take steps to amend legislation or otherwise clarify that the threshold requirement applies in line with the standard.

It is recommended that Bosnia and Herzegovina take steps to amend legislation or otherwise ensure that the filing deadline is not more than 12 months from the end of the reporting fiscal year.

It is recommended that Bosnia and Herzegovina take steps to implement procedures to ensure compliance with its filing requirement.

These recommendations remain in place since the 2019/2020 peer review.

The exchange of information framework

Bosnia and Herzegovina has no bilateral relationships in place for the exchange of CbC reports nor processes to ensure that the exchange of information is conducted in a manner consistent with the terms of reference relating to the exchange of information framework.

It is recommended that Bosnia and Herzegovina take steps to have qualifying competent authority agreements in effect with jurisdictions of the Inclusive Framework which meet the confidentiality, consistency and appropriate use conditions and with which Bosnia and Herzegovina has an international exchange of information agreement in effect that allows for the automatic exchange of tax information.

It is recommended that Bosnia and Herzegovina take steps to implement the necessary processes or written procedures to ensure that the exchange of information is conducted in a manner consistent with the terms of reference relating to the exchange of information framework.

These recommendations remain in place since the 2019/2020 peer review.

Bosnia and Herzegovina's 2020/2021 peer review report included a recommendation that Bosnia and Herzegovina take steps to ensure that the number of reports received and exchanged are monitored. This information has been provided for this review and this recommendation is removed.

Appropriate use of CbC reports

Bosnia and Herzegovina does not yet have controls in place to ensure the appropriate use of CbC reports.

It is recommended that Bosnia and Herzegovina take steps to ensure that the appropriate use condition is met ahead of the first exchanges of information. This recommendation remains in place since the 2019/2020 peer review.

Botswana

Overview of CbC reporting requirements

Botswana has not yet introduced a requirement for the filing of CbC reports, as required under the BEPS Action 13 (CbC reporting) minimum standard.

Summary of recommendations

Area of implementation	Recommendations for improvement
Domestic legal and administrative framework	It is recommended that Botswana take steps to implement a domestic legal and administrative framework to impose and enforce CbC reporting requirements as soon as possible.
Exchange of information framework	It is recommended that Botswana take steps to have qualifying competent authority agreements in effect with jurisdictions of the Inclusive Framework that meet the confidentiality, consistency and appropriate use conditions and with which Botswana has an international exchange of information agreement in effect that allows for the automatic exchange of tax information. It is recommended that Botswana take steps to implement the necessary processes or written procedures to ensure that the exchange of information is conducted in a manner consistent with the terms of reference relating to the exchange of information framework.
Appropriate use	It is recommended that Botswana take steps to ensure that the appropriate use condition is met ahead of the first exchanges of information.

The domestic legal and administrative framework

Botswana does not yet have legislation in place to implement the BEPS Action 13 minimum standard.

It is recommended that Botswana take steps to implement a domestic legal and administrative framework to impose and enforce CbC reporting requirements as soon as possible. This recommendation remains in place since the 2018/2019 peer review.

The exchange of information framework

Botswana has no bilateral relationships in place for the exchange of CbC reports nor processes to ensure that the exchange of information is conducted in a manner consistent with the terms of reference relating to the exchange of information framework.

It is recommended that Botswana take steps to have qualifying competent authority agreements in effect with jurisdictions of the Inclusive Framework that meet the confidentiality, consistency and appropriate use conditions and with which Botswana has an international exchange of information agreement in effect that allows for the automatic exchange of tax information. This recommendation remains in place since the 2018/2019 peer review.

It is recommended that Botswana take steps to implement the necessary processes or written procedures to ensure that the exchange of information is conducted in a manner consistent with the terms of reference relating to the exchange of information framework. This recommendation remains in place since the 2018/2019 peer review.

Appropriate use of CbC reports

Botswana does not yet have controls in place to ensure the appropriate use of CbC reports.

It is recommended that Botswana take steps to ensure that the appropriate use condition is met ahead of the first exchanges of information. This recommendation remains in place since the 2018/2019 peer review.

Brazil

Overview of CbC reporting requirements

First reporting fiscal year: Commencing on or after 1 January 2016

Consolidated group revenue threshold: BRL 2.26 trillion

Filing deadline: 7 months following the end of the reporting fiscal year

Local filing required: Yes

Surrogate parent entity filing permitted: Yes

First review of the domestic legal framework: 2017/2018

Summary of recommendations

Area of implementation	Recommendations for improvement
Domestic legal and administrative framework	None.
Exchange of information framework	None.
Appropriate use	None.

The domestic legal and administrative framework

Brazil confirms that its rules have not changed and continue to be applied effectively. Brazil continues to meet all terms of reference.[1]

The exchange of information framework

Brazil confirms that its rules have not changed and continue to be applied effectively. Brazil continues to meet all terms of reference.

Appropriate use of CbC reports

Brazil confirms that its rules have not changed and continue to be applied effectively. Brazil continues to meet all terms of reference.

Note

[1] Brazil's 2017/2018 peer review included a general monitoring point relating to a specific process that would allow to take appropriate measures in case Brazil is notified by another jurisdiction that such other

jurisdiction has reason to believe that an error may have led to incorrect or incomplete information reporting by a Reporting Entity or that there is non-compliance of a Reporting Entity with respect to its obligation to file a CbC report. This monitoring point remains in place.

British Virgin Islands

Overview of CbC reporting requirements

First reporting fiscal year: Commencing on or after 1 January 2018

Consolidated group revenue threshold: EUR 750 million

Filing deadline: 12 months following the end of the reporting fiscal year

Local filing required: No

Surrogate parent entity filing permitted: Yes

First review of the domestic legal framework: 2018/2019

Summary of recommendations

Area of implementation	Recommendations for improvement
Domestic legal and administrative framework	None.
Exchange of information framework	None.
Appropriate use	Not reviewed.

The domestic legal and administrative framework

British Virgin Islands confirms that its rules have not changed and continue to be applied effectively. British Virgin Islands continues to meet all terms of reference.

The exchange of information framework

British Virgin Islands confirms that its rules have not changed and continue to be applied effectively. British Virgin Islands continues to meet all terms of reference.

Appropriate use of CbC reports

British Virgin Islands is a non-reciprocal jurisdiction and, as such, will not receive CbC reports submitted to tax authorities in other jurisdictions, and will not apply local filing. It is therefore not necessary for this peer review evaluation to reach any conclusions with respect to compliance with the terms of reference on appropriate use.

Brunei Darussalam

Overview of CbC reporting requirements

Brunei Darussalam has not yet introduced a requirement for the filing of CbC reports, as required under the BEPS Action 13 (CbC reporting) minimum standard.

Summary of recommendations

Area of implementation	Recommendations for improvement
Domestic legal and administrative framework	It is recommended that Brunei Darussalam take steps to implement a domestic legal and administrative framework to impose and enforce CbC reporting requirements as soon as possible.
Exchange of information framework	It is recommended that Brunei Darussalam take steps to have qualifying competent authority agreements in effect with jurisdictions of the Inclusive Framework that meet the confidentiality, consistency and appropriate use conditions and with which Brunei Darussalam has an international exchange of information agreement in effect that allows for the automatic exchange of tax information. It is recommended that Brunei Darussalam take steps to implement the necessary processes or written procedures to ensure that the exchange of information is conducted in a manner consistent with the terms of reference relating to the exchange of information framework.
Appropriate use	It is recommended that Brunei Darussalam take steps to ensure that the appropriate use condition is met ahead of the first exchanges of information.

The domestic legal and administrative framework

Brunei Darussalam does not yet have legislation in place to implement the BEPS Action 13 minimum standard.

It is recommended that Brunei Darussalam take steps to implement a domestic legal and administrative framework to impose and enforce CbC reporting requirements as soon as possible. This recommendation remains in place since the 2017/2018 peer review.

The exchange of information framework

Brunei Darussalam has no bilateral relationships in place for the exchange of CbC reports nor processes to ensure that the exchange of information is conducted in a manner consistent with the terms of reference relating to the exchange of information framework.

It is recommended that Brunei Darussalam take steps to have qualifying competent authority agreements in effect with jurisdictions of the Inclusive Framework that meet the confidentiality, consistency and appropriate use conditions and with which Brunei Darussalam has an international exchange of information agreement in effect that allows for the automatic exchange of tax information. This recommendation remains in place since the 2017/2018 peer review.

It is recommended that Brunei Darussalam take steps to implement the necessary processes or written procedures to ensure that the exchange of information is conducted in a manner consistent with the terms

of reference relating to the exchange of information framework. This recommendation remains in place since the 2018/2019 peer review.

Appropriate use of CbC reports

Brunei Darussalam does not yet have controls in place to ensure the appropriate use of CbC reports.

It is recommended that Brunei Darussalam take steps to ensure that the appropriate use condition is met ahead of the first exchanges of information. This recommendation remains in place since the 2017/2018 peer review.

Bulgaria

Overview of CbC reporting requirements

First reporting fiscal year: Commencing on or after 1 January 2016

Consolidated group revenue threshold: EUR 750 million

Filing deadline: 12 months following the end of the reporting fiscal year

Local filing required: Yes, for reporting fiscal years commencing on or after 1 January 2017

Surrogate parent entity filing permitted: Yes

First review of the domestic legal framework: 2017/2018

Summary of recommendations

Area of implementation	Recommendations for improvement
Domestic legal and administrative framework	None.
Exchange of information framework	None.
Appropriate use	None.

The domestic legal and administrative framework

Bulgaria confirms that its rules have not changed and continue to be applied effectively. Bulgaria continues to meet all terms of reference.

The exchange of information framework

Bulgaria made some exchanges of CbC reports after the deadline. This was caused by a technical issue which has since been resolved and so no recommendation is required.

Bulgaria confirms that its rules have not changed and continue to be applied effectively. Bulgaria continues to meet all terms of reference.

Appropriate use of CbC reports

Bulgaria confirms that its rules have not changed and continue to be applied effectively. Bulgaria continues to meet all terms of reference.

Burkina Faso

Overview of CbC reporting requirements

First reporting fiscal year: Commencing on or after 1 January 2023

Consolidated group revenue threshold: XOF 491 billion

Filing deadline: 12 months following the end of the reporting fiscal year

Local filing required: Yes

Surrogate parent entity filing permitted: Yes

First review of the domestic legal framework: 2022/2023

Summary of recommendations

Area of implementation	Recommendations for improvement
Domestic legal and administrative framework	It is recommended that Burkina Faso introduce or complete the definitions of a "Group", "MNE Group", "Constituent Entity", "Consolidated Financial Statements", "Fiscal Year", "Reporting Fiscal Year", "Reporting Entity", and "Systemic Failure" in a manner that is consistent with the terms of reference.
	It is recommended that Burkina Faso publish the full content and format requirements of the CbC Report.
	It is recommended that Burkina Faso take steps to ensure that local filing only occurs in the circumstances permitted under the minimum standard.
	It is recommended that Burkina Faso clarify that the annual consolidated group revenue threshold calculation rule applies in line with the OECD guidance on currency fluctuations in respect of an MNE Group whose Ultimate Parent Entity is located in a jurisdiction other than Burkina Faso.
	It is recommended that Burkina Faso amend its legislation or otherwise take steps to ensure that enforcement provisions and monitoring relating to CbC reporting's effective implementation are provided for as contained in the terms of reference as from the first reporting period.
Exchange of information framework	It is recommended that Burkina Faso take steps to have qualifying competent authority agreements in effect with jurisdictions of the Inclusive Framework that meet the confidentiality, consistency and appropriate use conditions and with which Thailand has an international exchange of information agreement in effect that allows for the automatic exchange of tax information.
	It is recommended that Burkina Faso take steps to implement the necessary processes or written procedures to ensure that the exchange of information is conducted in a manner consistent with the terms of reference relating to the exchange of information framework.
Appropriate use	It is recommended that Burkina Faso take steps to ensure that the appropriate use condition is met ahead of the first exchanges of information.

The domestic legal and administrative framework

Burkina Faso has a number of recommendations to improve the legislation. These recommendations remain in place since the 2022/2023 peer review[1].

The definition of Group

Burkina Faso's legislation does not include a definition of "Group". It is recommended that Burkina Faso amend its legislation to include a definition of "Group" that is in line with the standard.

The definition of MNE Group

Burkina Faso's legislation does not include a definition of "MNE Group". It is recommended that Burkina Faso amend its legislation to include a definition of "MNE Group" that is in line with the standard.

The definition of Constituent Entity

Burkina Faso's legislation does not include a definition of "Constituent Entity". It is recommended that Burkina Faso amend its legislation to include a definition of "Constituent Entity" that is in line with the standard.

The definition of Consolidated Financial Statements

Burkina Faso's legislation does not include a definition of "Consolidated Financial Statements". It is recommended that Burkina Faso amend its legislation to include a definition of "Consolidated Financial Statements" that is in line with the standard.

The definition of Fiscal Year

Burkina Faso's legislation does not include a definition of "Fiscal Year". It is recommended that Burkina Faso amend its legislation to include a definition of "Fiscal Year" that is in line with the standard.

The definition of Reporting Fiscal Year

Burkina Faso's legislation does not include a definition of "Reporting Fiscal Year". It is recommended that Burkina Faso amend its legislation to include a definition of "Reporting Fiscal Year" that is in line with the standard.

The definition of Reporting Entity

Burkina Faso's legislation does not include a definition of "Reporting Entity". It is recommended that Burkina Faso amend its legislation to include a definition of "Reporting Entity" that is in line with the standard.

The definition of Systemic Failure

Burkina Faso's legislation does not include a definition of "Systemic Failure". It is recommended that Burkina Faso amend its legislation to include a definition of "Systemic Failure" that is in line with the standard.

Contents of the Country-by-Country report

The information included in Burkina Faso's legislation does not include the template of the Country-by-Country report and does not include any details of what should be included under each heading in the report. It is recommended that Burkina Faso publish the full content and format requirements of the CbC Report.

The local filing provision

Burkina Faso has a legislative requirement for local filing which is in effect despite Burkina Faso not yet meeting all of the consistency, confidentiality and appropriate use conditions. It is therefore recommended that Burkina Faso take steps to ensure that local filing only occurs in the circumstances permitted under the minimum standard.

Currency fluctuations

Where an MNE Group draws up, or would draw up, its Consolidated Financial Statements in a currency other than that specified by Burkina Faso, the reference to Burkina Faso's threshold has the effect as if it were a reference to the equivalent in that currency at the average exchange rate for the accounting period. While this provision would not create an issue for MNE Groups whose Ultimate Parent Entity is a tax resident in Burkina Faso, it may be incompatible with the guidance on currency fluctuations for MNE Groups whose Ultimate Parent Entity is located in another jurisdiction, if local filing requirements were applied in respect of a Constituent Entity (which is a Burkina Faso tax resident) of an MNE Group which does not reach the threshold as determined in the jurisdiction of the Ultimate Parent Entity of such a Group. It is recommended that Burkina Faso clarify that the annual consolidated group revenue threshold calculation rule applies in line with the OECD guidance on currency fluctuations in respect of an MNE Group whose Ultimate Parent Entity is located in a jurisdiction other than Burkina Faso.

Effective implementation

Burkina Faso does not have a legal mechanism in place to enforce compliance with the minimum standard. It is recommended that Burkina Faso take steps to ensure that enforcement provisions and monitoring relating to the enforcement of CbCR filing obligations are implemented.

The exchange of information framework

Burkina Faso has no bilateral relationships in place for the exchange of CbC reports nor processes to ensure that the exchange of information is conducted in a manner consistent with the terms of reference relating to the exchange of information framework.

It is recommended that Burkina Faso take steps to have qualifying competent authority agreements in effect with jurisdictions of the Inclusive Framework that meet the confidentiality, consistency and appropriate use conditions and with which Burkina Faso has an international exchange of information agreement in effect that allows for the automatic exchange of tax information. This recommendation remains in place since the 2022/2023 peer review.

It is recommended that Burkina Faso take steps to implement the necessary processes or written procedures to ensure that the exchange of information is conducted in a manner consistent with the terms of reference relating to the exchange of information framework. This recommendation remains in place since the 2022/2023 peer review.

Appropriate use of CbC reports

Burkina Faso does not yet have controls in place to ensure the appropriate use of CbC reports.

It is recommended that Burkina Faso take steps to ensure that the appropriate use condition is met ahead of the first exchanges of information. This recommendation remains in place since the 2022/2023 peer review.

Note

[1] Burkina Faso's 2022/2023 peer review included a general monitoring point relating to a specific process to that would allow to take appropriate measures in case Burkina Faso is notified by another jurisdiction that such other jurisdiction has reason to believe that an error may have led to incorrect or incomplete information reporting by a Reporting Entity or that there is non-compliance of a Reporting Entity with respect to its obligation to file a CbC report. This monitoring point remains in place.

Cabo Verde

Overview of CbC reporting requirements

First reporting fiscal year: TBC

Consolidated group revenue threshold: EUR 750 million

Filing deadline: 12 months following the end of the reporting fiscal year

Local filing required: Yes

Surrogate parent entity filing permitted: No

First review of domestic legal framework: 2021/2022

Summary of recommendations

Area of implementation	Recommendations for improvement
Domestic legal and administrative framework	It is recommended that Cabo Verde amend the definition of effective date or otherwise clarify the definition to be in line with the standard. It is recommended that Cabo Verde take steps to ensure that local filing only occurs in the circumstances permitted under the minimum standard. It is recommended that Cabo Verde clarify that the annual consolidated group revenue threshold calculation rule applies in line with the OECD guidance on currency fluctuations in respect of an MNE Group whose Ultimate Parent Entity is located in a jurisdiction other than Cabo Verde. The report includes a recommendation that Cabo Verde publish the full content and format requirements of the CbC Report.
Exchange of information framework	It is recommended that Cabo Verde take steps to have qualifying competent authority agreements in effect with jurisdictions of the Inclusive Framework that meet the confidentiality, consistency and appropriate use conditions and with which Cabo Verde has an international exchange of information agreement in effect that allows for the automatic exchange of tax information. It is recommended that Cabo Verde take steps to implement the necessary processes or written procedures to ensure that the exchange of information is conducted in a manner consistent with the terms of reference relating to the exchange of information framework.
Appropriate use	It is recommended that Cabo Verde take steps to ensure that the appropriate use condition is met ahead of the first exchanges of information.

The domestic legal and administrative framework

Cabo Verde has a number of recommendations to improve the legislation. These recommendations remain in place since the 2021/2022 peer review.

The definition of effective date

Cabo Verde's legislation does not include a definition of the effective date from which CbC reporting is required. It is recommended that Cabo Verde amend the legislation to include an effective date for the CbC filing requirement.

The local filing provision

The local filing definition in Cabo Verde's legislation applies to "The constituent entity…which is not the final parent entity of a group of multinational companies" and the legislative definition of multinational enterprise group does not specifically exclude groups which do not meet the threshold requirement. This can be read as requiring constituent entities of all MNE groups of any size to make a local filing if the conditions are met and is therefore too broad. It is recommended that Cabo Verde amend the definition of MNE groups to specify that it does include excluded MNE groups, or to otherwise specify a threshold requirement for local filing.

The first condition in Cabo Verde's legislation for local filing says: "The constituent entity residing in Cabo Verde […] are owned or controlled, directly or indirectly, by non-resident entities that are not required to submit an identical declaration". This is not in line with the condition to allow local filing, where the UPE of the group is not obligated to file a country-by-country report in its jurisdiction of tax residence. The condition contained in Cabo Verde's legislation is too broad and can be read as covering situations such as where there is a filing requirement in the other jurisdiction but the ultimate parent entity is not caught by that requirement because it is below the threshold. The intention is that this condition should apply where there is no filing requirement, not just where the ultimate parent entity is not required to file. It is recommended that Cabo Verde amend the definition or otherwise clarify the definition to be in line with the standard.

Cabo Verde has a legislative requirement for local filing which is in line with the standard, but which is in effect despite Cabo Verde not yet meeting all of the consistency, confidentiality and appropriate use conditions. It is therefore recommended that Cabo Verde take steps to ensure that local filing only occurs in the circumstances permitted under the minimum standard.

Currency Fluctuations

Where an MNE Group draws up, or would draw up, its Consolidated Financial Statements in a currency other than that specified by Cabo Verde, the reference to Cabo Verde's threshold has the effect as if it were a reference to the equivalent in that currency at the average exchange rate for the accounting period. While this provision would not create an issue for MNE Groups whose Ultimate Parent Entity is a tax resident in Cabo Verde, it may be incompatible with the guidance on currency fluctuations for MNE Groups whose Ultimate Parent Entity is located in another jurisdiction, if local filing requirements were applied in respect of a Constituent Entity (which is a Cabo Verde tax resident) of an MNE Group which does not reach the threshold as determined in the jurisdiction of the Ultimate Parent Entity of such a Group.

It is recommended that Cabo Verde clarify that the annual consolidated group revenue threshold calculation rule applies in line with the OECD guidance on currency fluctuations in respect of an MNE Group whose Ultimate Parent Entity is located in a jurisdiction other than Cabo Verde.

Contents of the Country-by-Country report

The information included in the legislative Annex does not include all of the template of the Country-by-Country report and does not include any details of what should be included under each heading in the report. The report includes a recommendation that Cabo Verde publish the full content and format requirements of the CbC Report.

The exchange of information framework

Cabo Verde has no bilateral relationships in place for the exchange of CbC reports nor processes to ensure that the exchange of information is conducted in a manner consistent with the terms of reference relating to the exchange of information framework.

It is recommended that Cabo Verde take steps to have qualifying competent authority agreements in effect with jurisdictions of the Inclusive Framework that meet the confidentiality, consistency and appropriate use conditions and with which Cabo Verde has an international exchange of information agreement in effect that allows for the automatic exchange of tax information. This recommendation remains in place since the 2019/2020 peer review.

It is recommended that Cabo Verde take steps to implement the necessary processes or written procedures to ensure that the exchange of information is conducted in a manner consistent with the terms of reference relating to the exchange of information framework. This recommendation remains in place since the 2019/2020 peer review.

Appropriate use of CbC reports

Cabo Verde does not yet have controls in place to ensure the appropriate use of CbC reports.

It is recommended that Cabo Verde take steps to ensure that the appropriate use condition is met ahead of the first exchanges of information. This recommendation remains in place since the 2019/2020 peer review.

Cameroon

Overview of CbC reporting requirements

First reporting fiscal year: Commencing on or after 1 January 2024

Consolidated group revenue threshold: XAF 492 billion

Filing deadline: 12 months following the end of the reporting fiscal year

Local filing required: Yes

Surrogate parent entity filing permitted: Yes

First review of domestic legal framework: 2023/2024.

Summary of recommendations

Area of implementation	Recommendations for improvement
Domestic legal and administrative framework	It is recommended that Cameroon introduce or complete the definitions of a "Group", "MNE Group", "Constituent Entity", "Consolidated Financial Statements", "Fiscal Year", "Reporting Entity" and "Systemic Failure" in a manner that is consistent with the terms of reference. It is recommended that Cameroon publish the full content and format requirements of the CbC Report. It is recommended that Cameroon take steps to ensure that local filing only occurs in the circumstances permitted under the minimum standard. It is recommended that Cameroon clarify that the annual consolidated group revenue threshold calculation rule applies in line with the OECD guidance on currency fluctuations in respect of an MNE Group whose Ultimate Parent Entity is located in a jurisdiction other than Cameroon.
Exchange of information framework	It is recommended that Cameroon take steps to have qualifying competent authority agreements in effect with jurisdictions of the Inclusive Framework that meet the confidentiality, consistency and appropriate use conditions and with which Cameroon has an international exchange of information agreement in effect that allows for the automatic exchange of tax information. It is recommended that Cameroon take steps to implement the necessary processes or written procedures to ensure that the exchange of information is conducted in a manner consistent with the terms of reference relating to the exchange of information framework.
Appropriate use	It is recommended that Cameroon take steps to ensure that the appropriate use condition is met ahead of the first exchanges of information.

The domestic legal and administrative framework

Cameroon's 2017/2018 peer review report included a recommendation to take steps to implement legislation to impose a CbC reporting filing requirement. Cameroon has since introduced such a filing requirement and this recommendation is removed.[1]

A CbC reporting filing obligation applies in Cameroon for fiscal years beginning on or after 1 January 2024 and filing is required 12 months after the reporting year end. Cameroon has enforcement requirements to ensure compliance with rules on CbC reporting.

There are a number of areas where there are recommendations to improve the legislation.

The definition of Group

Cameroon's legislation does not include a definition of "Group". It is recommended that Cameroon amend its legislation to include a definition of "Group" that is in line with the standard.

The definition of MNE Group

Cameroon's legislation does not include a definition of "MNE Group". It is recommended that Cameroon amend its legislation to include a definition of "MNE Group" that is in line with the standard.

The definition of Constituent Entity

Cameroon's legislation does not include a definition of "Constituent Entity". It is recommended that Cameroon amend its legislation to include a definition of "Constituent Entity" that is in line with the standard.

The definition of Consolidated Financial Statements

Cameroon's legislation does not include a definition of "Consolidated Financial Statements". It is recommended that Cameroon amend its legislation to include a definition of "Consolidated Financial Statements" that is in line with the standard.

The definition of Fiscal Year

Cameroon's legislation does not include a definition of "Fiscal Year". It is recommended that Cameroon amend its legislation to include a definition of "Fiscal Year" that is in line with the standard.

The definition of Reporting Entity

Cameroon's legislation does not include a definition of "Reporting Entity". It is recommended that Cameroon amend its legislation to include a definition of "Reporting Entity" that is in line with the standard.

The definition of Systemic Failure

Cameroon's legislation does not include a definition of "Systemic Failure". It is recommended that Cameroon amend its legislation to include a definition of "Systemic Failure" that is in line with the standard.

Contents of the Country-by-Country report

The information included in the legislation does not include all of the template of the Country-by-Country report and does not include any details of what should be included under each heading in the report. It is recommended that Cameroon publish the full content and format requirements of the CbC Report.

The local filing provision

Cameroon has a legislative requirement which is in effect despite Cameroon not yet meeting all of the consistency, confidentiality and appropriate use conditions. It is therefore recommended that Cameroon take steps to ensure that local filing only occurs in the circumstances permitted under the minimum standard.

Currency Fluctuations

Where an MNE Group draws up, or would draw up, its Consolidated Financial Statements in a currency other than that specified by Cameroon, the reference to Cameroon's threshold has the effect as if it were a reference to the equivalent in that currency at the average exchange rate for the accounting period. While this provision would not create an issue for MNE Groups whose Ultimate Parent Entity is a tax resident in Cameroon, it may be incompatible with the guidance on currency fluctuations for MNE Groups whose Ultimate Parent Entity is located in another jurisdiction, if local filing requirements were applied in respect of a Constituent Entity (which is a Cameroon tax resident) of an MNE Group which does not reach the threshold as determined in the jurisdiction of the Ultimate Parent Entity of such a Group.

It is recommended that Cameroon clarify that the annual consolidated group revenue threshold calculation rule applies in line with the OECD guidance on currency fluctuations in respect of an MNE Group whose Ultimate Parent Entity is located in a jurisdiction other than Cameroon.

The exchange of information framework

Cameroon has no bilateral relationships in place for the exchange of CbC reports nor processes to ensure that the exchange of information is conducted in a manner consistent with the terms of reference relating to the exchange of information framework.

It is recommended that Cameroon take steps to have qualifying competent authority agreements in effect with jurisdictions of the Inclusive Framework that meet the confidentiality, consistency and appropriate use conditions and with which Cameroon has an international exchange of information agreement in effect that allows for the automatic exchange of tax information. This recommendation remains in place since the 2017/2018 peer review.

It is recommended that Cameroon take steps to implement the necessary processes or written procedures to ensure that the exchange of information is conducted in a manner consistent with the terms of reference relating to the exchange of information framework. This recommendation remains in place since the 2018/2019 peer review.

Appropriate use of CbC reports

Cameroon does not yet have controls in place to ensure the appropriate use of CbC reports.

It is recommended that Cameroon take steps to ensure that the appropriate use condition is met ahead of the first exchanges of information. This recommendation remains in place since the 2017/2018 peer review.

Note

[1] https://www.prc.cm/fr/multimedia/documents/9875-loi-n-2023-019-du-19-12-2023

Canada

Overview of CbC reporting requirements

First reporting fiscal year: Commencing on or after 1 January 2016

Consolidated group revenue threshold: EUR 750 million

Filing deadline: 12 months following the end of the reporting fiscal year

Local filing required: Yes

Surrogate parent entity filing permitted: Yes

First review of the domestic legal framework: 2017/2018

Summary of recommendations

Area of implementation	Recommendations for improvement
Domestic legal and administrative framework	None.
Exchange of information framework	None.
Appropriate use	None.

The domestic legal and administrative framework

Canada confirms that its rules have not changed and continue to be applied effectively. Canada continues to meet all terms of reference.

The exchange of information framework

Canada confirms that its rules have not changed and continue to be applied effectively. Canada continues to meet all terms of reference.

Appropriate use of CbC reports

Canada confirms that its rules have not changed and continue to be applied effectively. Canada continues to meet all terms of reference.

Cayman Islands

Overview of CbC reporting requirements

First reporting fiscal year: Commencing on or after 1 January 2016

Consolidated group revenue threshold: USD 850 million

Filing deadline: 12 months following the end of the reporting fiscal year

Local filing required: No

Surrogate parent entity filing permitted: Yes

First review of the domestic legal framework: 2017/2018

Summary of recommendations

Area of implementation	Recommendations for improvement
Domestic legal and administrative framework	None.
Exchange of information framework	None.
Appropriate use	Not reviewed.

The domestic legal and administrative framework

The Cayman Islands confirms that its rules have not changed and continue to be applied effectively. The Cayman Islands continues to meet all terms of reference.

The exchange of information framework

The Cayman Islands confirms that its rules have not changed and continue to be applied effectively. The Cayman Islands continues to meet all terms of reference.

Appropriate use of CbC reports

The Cayman Islands is a non-reciprocal jurisdiction and, as such, will not receive CbC reports submitted to tax authorities in other jurisdictions, and will not apply local filing. It is therefore not necessary for this peer review evaluation to reach any conclusions with respect to the Cayman Islands' compliance with the terms of reference on appropriate use.

Chile

Overview of CbC reporting requirements

First reporting fiscal year: Commencing on or after 1 January 2016

Consolidated group revenue threshold: EUR 750 million

Filing deadline: 6 months following the end of the reporting fiscal year

Local filing required: No

Surrogate parent entity filing permitted: Yes

First review of the domestic legal framework: 2017/2018

Summary of recommendations

Area of implementation	Recommendations for improvement
Domestic legal and administrative framework	None.
Exchange of information framework	None.
Appropriate use	None.

The domestic legal and administrative framework

Chile confirms that its rules have not changed and continue to be applied effectively. Chile continues to meet all terms of reference.

The exchange of information framework

Chile notified some late exchanges of CbC reports after the deadline, due to error. Chile has introduced measures to address the issue underlying this error. As Chile has taken steps to address this issue, no recommendation is made but this aspect will be monitored.

Chile confirms that its rules have not changed and continue to be applied effectively. Chile continues to meet all terms of reference.

Appropriate use of CbC reports

Chile confirms that its rules have not changed and continue to be applied effectively. Chile continues to meet all terms of reference.

China (People's Republic of)

Overview of CbC reporting requirements

First reporting fiscal year: Commencing on or after 1 January 2016

Consolidated group revenue threshold: RMB 5.5 billion

Filing deadline: 5 months following the end of the reporting fiscal year

Local filing required: Yes

Surrogate parent entity filing permitted: Yes

First review of the domestic legal framework: 2017/2018

Summary of recommendations

Area of implementation	Recommendations for improvement
Domestic legal and administrative framework	It is recommendation that China clarify the exact scope, conditions and legal basis under the minimum standard and/or the exchange of information framework for the filing exemption in relation to information relating to National Security. It is recommended that China amend its legislation or otherwise takes steps to ensure that local filing is only required in the circumstances contained in the terms of reference.
Exchange of information framework	None.
Appropriate use	None.

The domestic legal and administrative framework

It is recommendation that China clarify the exact scope, conditions and legal basis under the minimum standard and/or the exchange of information framework for the filing exemption in relation to information relating to National Security. This recommendation remains in place since the 2017/2018 peer review.

It is recommended that China amend its legislation or otherwise takes steps to ensure that local filing is only required in the circumstances contained in the terms of reference. This recommendation remains in place since the 2017/2018 peer review.

The exchange of information framework

China's 2021/2022 peer review included a monitoring point relating to a technical issue with one particular batch of reports and which was being investigated by both parties to the exchange. The issue has now been resolved and so this monitoring point is now removed.

China confirms that its rules have not changed and continue to be applied effectively. China continues to meet all terms of reference.

Appropriate use of CbC reports

China confirms that its rules have not changed and continue to be applied effectively. China continues to meet all terms of reference.

Colombia

Overview of CbC reporting requirements

First reporting fiscal year: Commencing on or after 1 January 2016

Consolidated group revenue threshold: UVT 81 million (Tax Value Units)

Filing deadline: 12 months following the end of the reporting fiscal year

Local filing required: Yes

Surrogate parent entity filing permitted: Yes

First review of the domestic legal framework: 2017/2018

Summary of recommendations

Area of implementation	Recommendations for improvement
Domestic legal and administrative framework	None.
Exchange of information framework	None.
Appropriate use	None.

The domestic legal and administrative framework

Colombia confirms that its rules have not changed and continue to be applied effectively. Colombia continues to meet all terms of reference.

The exchange of information framework

Colombia confirms that its rules have not changed and continue to be applied effectively. Colombia continues to meet all terms of reference.

Appropriate use of CbC reports

Colombia confirms that its rules have not changed and continue to be applied effectively. Colombia continues to meet all terms of reference.

Congo

Overview of CbC reporting requirements

First reporting fiscal year: Beginning on or after 1 January 2023

Consolidated group revenue threshold: entity revenues or gross assets of XAF 500 million

Filing deadline: Within 6 months following the filing of the annual income tax return

Local filing required: Yes

Surrogate parent entity filing permitted: No

First review of domestic legal framework: 2023/2024

Summary of recommendations

Area of implementation	Recommendations for improvement
Domestic legal and administrative framework	It is recommended that Congo take steps to amend the filing threshold or otherwise clarify that it is in line with the standard. It is recommended that Congo takes steps to amend its legislation or otherwise clarify that an MNE Group should consider its requirement to file using the consolidated group revenue of its fiscal year immediately preceding a reporting fiscal year for comparison with the threshold. It is recommended that Congo take steps to amend its legislation or otherwise ensure that the content required in the CbC Report is in line with the minimum standard. It is recommended that Congo publish the full content and format requirements of the CbC Report. It is recommended that Congo take steps to ensure that local filing only occurs in the circumstances permitted under the minimum standard. It is recommended that Congo take steps to amend its legislation or otherwise impose a limitation on local filing in case of surrogate filing in line with the standard. It is recommended that Congo clarify that the annual consolidated group revenue threshold calculation rule applies in line with the OECD guidance on currency fluctuations in respect of an MNE Group whose Ultimate Parent Entity is located in a jurisdiction other than Congo. It is recommended that Congo implement a provision whereby a single Constituent Entity of the same MNE Group may be designated to file the CbC report which would satisfy the local filing requirement of all the Constituent Entities in Congo.
Exchange of information framework	It is recommended that Congo take steps to have qualifying competent authority agreements in effect with jurisdictions of the Inclusive Framework that meet the confidentiality, consistency and appropriate use conditions and with which Congo has an international exchange of information agreement in effect that allows for the automatic exchange of tax information. It is recommended that Congo take steps to implement the necessary processes or written procedures to ensure that the exchange of information is conducted in a manner consistent with the terms of reference relating to the exchange of information framework.
Appropriate use	It is recommended that Congo take steps to ensure that the appropriate use condition is met ahead of the first exchanges of information.

The domestic legal and administrative framework

Congo's 2019/2020 peer review report included a recommendation to take steps to implement legislation to impose a CbC reporting filing requirement. Congo has since introduced such a filing requirement and this recommendation is removed.[1]

A CbC reporting filing obligation applies in Congo for fiscal years beginning on or after 1 January 2023 and filing is required within 6 months following the filing of the annual income tax return (10 months and 20 days after the reporting year-end). Congo has enforcement requirements to ensure compliance with rules on CbC reporting.

There are a number of areas where there are recommendations to improve the legislation.

Filing Threshold

Congo's legislation specifies a filing threshold of XAF 500 million of local entity revenue or gross assets. The minimum standard requires a filing threshold of EUR 750 million or a near equivalent amount in domestic currency as of January 2015. The filing threshold specified in Congo's legislation is not consistent with this. It is recommended that Congo take steps to amend the filing threshold or otherwise clarify that it is in line with the standard.

Reporting fiscal year

Congo's legislation does not specify that the threshold requirement refers to MNE Groups' consolidated group revenue of its immediately preceding fiscal year. It is recommended that Congo takes steps to amend legislation or otherwise clarify that an MNE Group should consider its requirement to file using the consolidated group revenue of its fiscal year immediately preceding a reporting fiscal year for comparison with the threshold.

Contents of the Country-by-Country report

Congo's legislation outlines the content of the CbC report but there are several areas in which this does not correspond with the terms of reference. The legislation does not require information on Constituent Entities which do not have a controlled transaction with a Constituent Entity resident in Congo. The legislation also requires the CbC report to include information on the financial years to which retained earnings relate, which is not required under the minimum standard. It is recommended that Congo take steps to amend legislation or otherwise ensure that the content required in the CbC report is in line with the standard.

The information included in the legislation does not include all of the template of the Country-by-Country report and does not include any details of what should be included under each heading in the report. It is recommended that Congo publish the full content and format requirements of the CbC report.

The local filing provision

The local filing provision in Congo applies where an MNE Group has a Constituent Entity established in Congo which has revenues or gross assets in excess of the threshold. This is broader than the condition under the standard, where a jurisdiction may require local filing where one or more of the following conditions have been met with respect to that fiscal year: (a) Ultimate Parent Entity of the MNE Group is not obligated to file a Country-by-Country Report in its jurisdiction of tax residence; or (b) the jurisdiction in which the Ultimate Parent Entity is resident for tax purposes has a current International Agreement to which the given jurisdiction is a party but does not have a Qualifying Competent Authority Agreement in effect to which this jurisdiction is a party by the time for filing the Country-by-Country Report; or (c) there has been a Systemic Failure of the jurisdiction of tax residence of the Ultimate Parent Entity that has been notified to the Constituent Entity by its tax administration. It is recommended that Congo take steps to ensure that local filing only occurs in the circumstances permitted under the minimum standard.

Congo has a legislative requirement which is in effect despite Congo not yet meeting all of the consistency, confidentiality and appropriate use conditions. It is therefore recommended that Congo take steps to ensure that local filing only occurs in the circumstances permitted under the minimum standard.

Limitation on local filing in case of surrogate filing

Congo's legislation does not limit local filing in case of surrogate filing. It is recommended that Congo take steps to amend its legislation or otherwise impose a limitation on local filing in case of surrogate filing in line with the standard.

Currency Fluctuations

Where an MNE Group draws up, or would draw up, its Consolidated Financial Statements in a currency other than that specified by a jurisdiction, the reference to the jurisdiction's threshold has the effect as if it were a reference to the equivalent in that currency at the average exchange rate for the accounting period. While this provision would not create an issue for MNE Groups whose Ultimate Parent Entity is a tax resident in that jurisdiction, it may be incompatible with the guidance on currency fluctuations for MNE Groups whose Ultimate Parent Entity is located in another jurisdiction, if local filing requirements were applied in respect of a Constituent Entity (which is a tax resident of the first jurisdiction) of an MNE Group which does not reach the threshold as determined in the jurisdiction of the Ultimate Parent Entity of such a Group. It is recommended that Congo clarify that the threshold calculation rule applies in line with the OECD guidance on currency fluctuations in respect of an MNE Group whose Ultimate Parent Entity is located in a jurisdiction other than Congo.

Single Entity Filing

It is recommended that Congo implement a provision whereby a single Constituent Entity of the same MNE Group may be designated to file the CbC report which would satisfy the local filing requirement of all the Constituent Entities in Congo.

The exchange of information framework

Congo has no bilateral relationships in place for the exchange of CbC reports nor processes to ensure that the exchange of information is conducted in a manner consistent with the terms of reference relating to the exchange of information framework.

It is recommended that Congo take steps to have qualifying competent authority agreements in effect with jurisdictions of the Inclusive Framework that meet the confidentiality, consistency and appropriate use conditions and with which Congo has an international exchange of information agreement in effect that allows for the automatic exchange of tax information. This recommendation remains in place since the 2019/2020 peer review.

It is recommended that Congo take steps to implement the necessary processes or written procedures to ensure that the exchange of information is conducted in a manner consistent with the terms of reference relating to the exchange of information framework. This recommendation remains in place since the 2019/2020 peer review.

Appropriate use of CbC reports

Congo does not yet have controls in place to ensure the appropriate use of CbC reports.

It is recommended that Congo take steps to ensure that the appropriate use condition is met ahead of the first exchanges of information. This recommendation remains in place since the 2019/2020 peer review.

Note

[1] https://www.finances.gouv.cg/sites/default/files/documents/LF 2023.pdf

Costa Rica

Overview of CbC reporting requirements

First reporting fiscal year: Commencing on or after 1 January 2017

Consolidated group revenue threshold: EUR 750 million

Filing deadline: 31 December of the year following the reporting fiscal year

Local filing required: No

Surrogate parent entity filing permitted: Yes

First review of the domestic legal framework: 2017/2018

Summary of recommendations

Area of implementation	Recommendations for improvement
Domestic legal and administrative framework	None.
Exchange of information framework	None.
Appropriate use	None.

The domestic legal and administrative framework

Costa Rica confirms that its rules have not changed and continue to be applied effectively. Costa Rica continues to meet all terms of reference.

The exchange of information framework

Costa Rica's 2022/2023 peer review included a monitoring point relating to late exchanges. Costa Rica has introduced measures to address the issue underlying these late exchanges and so this monitoring point is now removed.

Costa Rica confirms that its rules have not changed and continue to be applied effectively. Costa Rica continues to meet all terms of reference.

Appropriate use of CbC reports

Costa Rica's 2022/2023 peer report did not reach any conclusions with regard to appropriate use of CbC reports as Costa Rica was a non-reciprocal jurisdiction. Costa Rica has now notified as a reciprocal jurisdiction.

Prior to becoming a non-reciprocal jurisdiction, Costa Rica had provided information that confirms that it has controls in place to ensure the appropriate use of CbC reports. Costa Rica confirms that these rules have not changed and continue to be applied effectively. Costa Rica meets all terms of reference.

Côte d'Ivoire

Overview of CbC reporting requirements

First reporting fiscal year: Commencing on or after 1 January 2018

Consolidated group revenue threshold: XOF 491 967 750 000

Filing deadline: 12 months following the end of the reporting fiscal year

Local filing required: No

Surrogate parent entity filing permitted: Yes

First review of the domestic legal framework: 2017/2018

Summary of recommendations

Area of implementation	Recommendations for improvement
Domestic legal and administrative framework	None.
Exchange of information framework	It is recommended that Côte d'Ivoire take steps to have qualifying competent authority agreements in effect with jurisdictions of the Inclusive Framework which meet the confidentiality, consistency and appropriate use conditions and with which Côte d'Ivoire has an international exchange of information agreement in effect that allows for the automatic exchange of tax information. It is also recommended that Côte d'Ivoire have in place the necessary processes or written procedures to ensure that the exchange of information is conducted in a manner consistent with the terms of reference relating to the exchange of information framework.
Appropriate use	It is recommended that Côte d'Ivoire take steps to ensure that the appropriate use condition is met ahead of the first exchanges of information.

The domestic legal and administrative framework

Côte d'Ivoire confirms that its rules have not changes and continue to be applied effectively. Côte d'Ivoire continues to meet all terms of reference.[1]

The exchange of information framework

Côte d'Ivoire has no bilateral relationships in place for the exchange of CbC reports nor processes to ensure that the exchange of information is conducted in a manner consistent with the terms of reference relating to the exchange of information framework.

It is recommended that Côte d'Ivoire take steps to have qualifying competent authority agreements in effect with jurisdictions of the Inclusive Framework which meet the confidentiality, consistency and appropriate use conditions and with which Côte d'Ivoire has an international exchange of information agreement in effect that allows for the automatic exchange of tax information. This recommendation remains in place since the 2017/2018 peer review.

It is recommended that Côte d'Ivoire have in place the necessary processes or written procedures to ensure that the exchange of information is conducted in a manner consistent with the terms of reference relating to the exchange of information framework. This recommendation remains in place since the 2018/2019 peer review.

Appropriate use of CbC reports

Côte d'Ivoire does not yet have controls in place to ensure the appropriate use of CbC reports.

It is recommended that Côte d'Ivoire take steps to ensure that the appropriate use condition is met ahead of the first exchanges of information. This recommendation remains in place since the 2017/2018 peer review.

Note

[1] Côte d'Ivoire's 2017/2018 peer review included a general monitoring point relating to a specific process to that would allow to take appropriate measures in case Côte d'Ivoire is notified by another jurisdiction that such other jurisdiction has reason to believe that an error may have led to incorrect or incomplete information reporting by a Reporting Entity or that there is non-compliance of a Reporting Entity with respect to its obligation to file a CbC report. This monitoring point remains in place.

Croatia

Overview of CbC reporting requirements

First reporting fiscal year: Commencing on or after 1 January 2016

Consolidated group revenue threshold: EUR 750 million

Filing deadline: 12 months following the end of the reporting fiscal year

Local filing required: Yes, for reporting fiscal years commencing on or after 1 January 2017

Surrogate parent entity filing permitted: Yes

First review of the domestic legal framework: 2017/2018

Summary of recommendations

Area of implementation	Recommendations for improvement
Domestic legal and administrative framework	None.
Exchange of information framework	None.
Appropriate use	None.

The domestic legal and administrative framework

Croatia confirms that its rules have not changed and continue to be applied effectively. Croatia continues to meet all terms of reference.

The exchange of information framework

Croatia confirms that its rules have not changed and continue to be applied effectively. Croatia continues to meet all terms of reference.

Appropriate use of CbC reports

Croatia confirms that its rules have not changed and continue to be applied effectively. Croatia continues to meet all terms of reference.

Curaçao

Overview of CbC reporting requirements

First reporting fiscal year: Commencing on or after 1 January 2018. Curaçao also allowed MNE Groups to file a CbC report on a voluntary basis, for reporting fiscal years commencing between 1 January 2016 and 31 December 2017.

Consolidated group revenue threshold: NAFI 1.5 billion

Filing deadline: 12 months following the end of the reporting fiscal year

Local filing required: No

Surrogate parent entity filing permitted: Yes

First review of the domestic legal framework: 2018/2019

Summary of recommendations

Area of implementation	Recommendations for improvement
Domestic legal and administrative framework	None.
Exchange of information framework	None.
Appropriate use	None.

The domestic legal and administrative framework

Curaçao confirms that its rules have not changed and continue to be applied effectively. Curaçao continues to meet all terms of reference.

The exchange of information framework

Curaçao's 2022/2023 peer report included a recommendation that Curaçao take steps to ensure that the number of reports received and exchanged are monitored. Curaçao has addressed this issue and this recommendation is removed.

Curaçao notified some late exchanges of CbC reports, due to a technical issue. This has now been fixed and so no recommendation has been made.

Curaçao confirms that its rules have not changed and continue to be applied effectively. Curaçao continues to meet all terms of reference.

Appropriate use of CbC reports

Curaçao's 2022/2023 report did not reach any conclusions with regard to appropriate use of CbC reports as Curaçao was a non-reciprocal jurisdiction. Curaçao has now notified as a reciprocal jurisdiction.

Curaçao has provided details of the controls it has in place to ensure the appropriate use of CbC reports, which comply with published Guidance on the Appropriate Use of Information Contained in CbC Reports.

Curaçao meets all terms of reference with respect to the appropriate use condition.

Czechia

Overview of CbC reporting requirements

First reporting fiscal year: Commencing on or after 1 January 2016

Consolidated group revenue threshold: EUR 750 million

Filing deadline: 12 months following the end of the reporting fiscal year

Local filing required: Yes, for reporting fiscal years commencing on or after 1 January 2017

Surrogate parent entity filing permitted: Yes

First review of the domestic legal framework: 2017/2018

Summary of recommendations

Area of implementation	Recommendations for improvement
Domestic legal and administrative framework	None.
Exchange of information framework	None.
Appropriate use	None.

The domestic legal and administrative framework

Czechia confirms that its rules have not changed and continue to be applied effectively. Czechia continues to meet all terms of reference.

The exchange of information framework

Czechia confirms that its rules have not changed and continue to be applied effectively. Czechia continues to meet all terms of reference.

Appropriate use of CbC reports

Czechia confirms that its rules have not changed and continue to be applied effectively. Czechia continues to meet all terms of reference.

Democratic Republic of the Congo

Overview of CbC reporting requirements

The Democratic Republic of the Congo has not yet introduced a requirement for the filing of CbC reports, as required under the BEPS Action 13 (CbC reporting) minimum standard.

Summary of recommendations

Area of implementation	Recommendations for improvement
Domestic legal and administrative framework	It is recommended that the Democratic Republic of the Congo take steps to implement a domestic legal and administrative framework to impose and enforce CbC reporting requirements as soon as possible.
Exchange of information framework	It is recommended that the Democratic Republic of the Congo take steps to have qualifying competent authority agreements in effect with jurisdictions of the Inclusive Framework that meet the confidentiality, consistency and appropriate use conditions and with which the Democratic Republic of the Congo has an international exchange of information agreement in effect that allows for the automatic exchange of tax information. It is recommended that the Democratic Republic of the Congo take steps to implement the necessary processes or written procedures to ensure that the exchange of information is conducted in a manner consistent with the terms of reference relating to the exchange of information framework.
Appropriate use	It is recommended that the Democratic Republic of the Congo take steps to ensure that the appropriate use condition is met ahead of the first exchanges of information.

The domestic legal and administrative framework

The Democratic Republic of the Congo does not yet have legislation in place to implement the BEPS Action 13 minimum standard.

It is recommended that the Democratic Republic of the Congo take steps to implement a domestic legal and administrative framework to impose and enforce CbC reporting requirements as soon as possible. This recommendation remains in place since the 2017/2018 peer review.

The exchange of information framework

The Democratic Republic of the Congo has no bilateral relationships in place for the exchange of CbC reports nor processes to ensure that the exchange of information is conducted in a manner consistent with the terms of reference relating to the exchange of information framework.

It is recommended that the Democratic Republic of the Congo take steps to have qualifying competent authority agreements in effect with jurisdictions of the Inclusive Framework that meet the confidentiality, consistency and appropriate use conditions and with which the Democratic Republic of the Congo has an international exchange of information agreement in effect that allows for the automatic exchange of tax information. This recommendation remains in place since the 2017/2018 peer review.

It is recommended that the Democratic Republic of the Congo take steps to implement the necessary processes or written procedures to ensure that the exchange of information is conducted in a manner consistent with the terms of reference relating to the exchange of information framework. This recommendation remains in place since the 2018/2019 peer review.

Appropriate use of CbC reports

The Democratic Republic of the Congo does not yet have controls in place to ensure the appropriate use of CbC reports.

It is recommended that the Democratic Republic of the Congo take steps to ensure that the appropriate use condition is met ahead of the first exchanges of information. This recommendation remains in place since the 2017/2018 peer review.

Denmark

Overview of CbC reporting requirements

First reporting fiscal year: Commencing on or after 1 January 2016

Consolidated group revenue threshold: DKK 5.6 billion

Filing deadline: 12 months following the end of the reporting fiscal year

Local filing required: Yes, for reporting fiscal years commencing on or after 1 January 2017

Surrogate parent entity filing permitted: Yes

First review of the domestic legal framework: 2017/2018

Summary of recommendations

Area of implementation	Recommendations for improvement
Domestic legal and administrative framework	None.
Exchange of information framework	None.
Appropriate use	None.

The domestic legal and administrative framework

Denmark confirms that its rules have not changed and continue to be applied effectively. Denmark continues to meet all terms of reference.

The exchange of information framework

Denmark confirms that its rules have not changed and continue to be applied effectively. Denmark continues to meet all terms of reference.

Appropriate use of CbC reports

Denmark confirms that its rules have not changed and continue to be applied effectively. Denmark continues to meet all terms of reference.

Djibouti

Overview of CbC reporting requirements

Djibouti has not yet introduced a requirement for the filing of CbC reports, as required under the BEPS Action 13 (CbC reporting) minimum standard.

Summary of recommendations

Area of implementation	Recommendations for improvement
Domestic legal and administrative framework	It is recommended that Djibouti take steps to implement a domestic legal and administrative framework to impose and enforce CbC reporting requirements as soon as possible.
Exchange of information framework	It is recommended that Djibouti take steps to have qualifying competent authority agreements in effect with jurisdictions of the Inclusive Framework that meet the confidentiality, consistency and appropriate use conditions and with which Djibouti has an international exchange of information agreement in effect that allows for the automatic exchange of tax information. It is recommended that Djibouti take steps to implement the necessary processes or written procedures to ensure that the exchange of information is conducted in a manner consistent with the terms of reference relating to the exchange of information framework.
Appropriate use	It is recommended that Djibouti take steps to ensure that the appropriate use condition is met ahead of the first exchanges of information.

The domestic legal and administrative framework

Djibouti does not yet have legislation in place to implement the BEPS Action 13 minimum standard.

It is recommended that Djibouti take steps to implement a domestic legal and administrative framework to impose and enforce CbC reporting requirements as soon as possible. This recommendation remains in place since the 2018/2019 peer review.

The exchange of information framework

Djibouti has no bilateral relationships in place for the exchange of CbC reports nor processes to ensure that the exchange of information is conducted in a manner consistent with the terms of reference relating to the exchange of information framework.

It is recommended that Djibouti take steps to have qualifying competent authority agreements in effect with jurisdictions of the Inclusive Framework that meet the confidentiality, consistency and appropriate use conditions and with which Djibouti has an international exchange of information agreement in effect that allows for the automatic exchange of tax information. This recommendation remains in place since the 2018/2019 peer review.

It is recommended that Djibouti take steps to implement the necessary processes or written procedures to ensure that the exchange of information is conducted in a manner consistent with the terms of reference relating to the exchange of information framework. This recommendation remains in place since the 2018/2019 peer review.

Appropriate use of CbC reports

Djibouti does not yet have controls in place to ensure the appropriate use of CbC reports.

It is recommended that Djibouti take steps to ensure that the appropriate use condition is met ahead of the first exchanges of information. This recommendation remains in place since the 2018/2019 peer review.

Dominica

Overview of CbC reporting requirements

Dominica has not yet introduced a requirement for the filing of CbC reports, as required under the BEPS Action 13 (CbC reporting) minimum standard.

Summary of recommendations

Area of implementation	Recommendations for improvement
Domestic legal and administrative framework	It is recommended that Dominica take steps to implement a domestic legal and administrative framework to impose and enforce CbC reporting requirements as soon as possible.
Exchange of information framework	It is recommended that Dominica take steps to have qualifying competent authority agreements in effect with jurisdictions of the Inclusive Framework that meet the confidentiality, consistency and appropriate use conditions and with which Dominica has an international exchange of information agreement in effect that allows for the automatic exchange of tax information. It is recommended that Dominica take steps to implement the necessary processes or written procedures to ensure that the exchange of information is conducted in a manner consistent with the terms of reference relating to the exchange of information framework.
Appropriate use	It is recommended that Dominica take steps to ensure that the appropriate use condition is met ahead of the first exchanges of information.

The domestic legal and administrative framework

Dominica does not yet have legislation in place to implement the BEPS Action 13 minimum standard.

It is recommended that Dominica take steps to implement a domestic legal and administrative framework to impose and enforce CbC reporting requirements as soon as possible. This recommendation remains in place since the 2019/2020 peer review.

The exchange of information framework

Dominica has no bilateral relationships in place for the exchange of CbC reports nor processes to ensure that the exchange of information is conducted in a manner consistent with the terms of reference relating to the exchange of information framework.

It is recommended that Dominica take steps to have qualifying competent authority agreements in effect with jurisdictions of the Inclusive Framework that meet the confidentiality, consistency and appropriate use conditions and with which Dominica has an international exchange of information agreement in effect that allows for the automatic exchange of tax information. This recommendation remains in place since the 2019/2020 peer review.

It is recommended that Dominica take steps to implement the necessary processes or written procedures to ensure that the exchange of information is conducted in a manner consistent with the terms of reference relating to the exchange of information framework. This recommendation remains in place since the 2019/2020 peer review.

Appropriate use of CbC reports

Dominica does not yet have controls in place to ensure the appropriate use of CbC reports.

It is recommended that Dominica take steps to ensure that the appropriate use condition is met ahead of the first exchanges of information. This recommendation remains in place since the 2019/2020 peer review.

Dominican Republic

Overview of CbC reporting requirements

Consolidated group revenue threshold: DOP 38.8 billion

Filing deadline: 12 months following the end of the reporting fiscal year

Local filing required: Yes

Surrogate parent entity filing permitted: Yes

First review of domestic legal framework: 2021/2022

Summary of recommendations

Area of implementation	Recommendations for improvement
Domestic legal and administrative framework	It is recommended that Dominican Republic take steps to ensure that local filing only occurs in the circumstances permitted under the minimum standard.
Exchange of information framework	It is recommended that Dominican Republic take steps to have qualifying competent authority agreements in effect with jurisdictions of the Inclusive Framework that meet the confidentiality, consistency and appropriate use conditions and with which the Dominican Republic has an international exchange of information agreement in effect that allows for the automatic exchange of tax information.
Appropriate use	None.

The domestic legal and administrative framework

It is recommended that Dominican Republic ensure that local filing only occurs in the circumstances permitted under the minimum standard. This recommendation remains in place since the 2021/2022 peer review.

The exchange of information framework

The Dominican Republic has no bilateral relationships in place for the exchange of CbC reports nor processes to ensure that the exchange of information is conducted in a manner consistent with the terms of reference relating to the exchange of information framework.

It is recommended that the Dominican Republic take steps to have qualifying competent authority agreements in effect with jurisdictions of the Inclusive Framework that meet the confidentiality, consistency and appropriate use conditions and with which the Dominican Republic has an international exchange of information agreement in effect that allows for the automatic exchange of tax information. This recommendation remains in place since the 2019/2020 peer review.

For information, Dominican Republic has implemented the necessary processes or written procedures to ensure that the exchange of information is conducted in a manner consistent with the terms of reference relating to the exchange of information framework.

Appropriate use of CbC reports

Dominican Republic confirms that its rules have not changed and continue to be applied effectively. Dominican Republic continues to meet all terms of reference.

Egypt

Overview of CbC reporting requirements

First reporting fiscal year: Ending on or after 31 December 2018

Consolidated group revenue threshold: EGP 3 billion

Filing deadline: 12 months following the end of the reporting fiscal year

Local filing required: No

Surrogate parent entity filing permitted: No

First review of the domestic legal framework: 2017/2018

Summary of recommendations

Area of implementation	Recommendations for improvement
Domestic legal and administrative framework	None.
Exchange of information framework	It is recommended that Egypt take steps to have qualifying competent authority agreements in effect with jurisdictions of the Inclusive Framework which meet the confidentiality, consistency and appropriate use conditions and with which Egypt has an international exchange of information agreement in effect that allows for the automatic exchange of tax information. It is recommended that Egypt take steps to implement processes or written procedures to ensure that the exchange of information is conducted in a manner consistent with the terms of reference relating to the exchange of information framework ahead of its first exchanges of information.
Appropriate use	It is recommended that Egypt take steps to ensure that the appropriate use condition is met ahead of the first exchanges of information.

The domestic legal and administrative framework

Egypt's 2022/2023 peer review included a recommendation that Egypt take steps to ensure that local filing only occurs in the circumstances permitted under the minimum standard. Egypt has clarified that there is no local filing requirement, and so this recommendation is removed.

Egypt's 2022/2023 peer review included a recommendation that Egypt clarify that the annual consolidated group revenue threshold calculation rule applies in line with the OECD guidance on currency fluctuations in respect of an MNE Group whose Ultimate Parent Entity is located in a jurisdiction other than Egypt. Egypt has clarified that there is no local filing requirement, meaning this guidance is not required. This recommendation is therefore removed.

The exchange of information framework

Egypt has no bilateral relationships in place for the exchange of CbC reports nor processes to ensure that the exchange of information is conducted in a manner consistent with the terms of reference relating to the exchange of information framework.

It is recommended that Egypt take steps to have qualifying competent authority agreements in effect with jurisdictions of the Inclusive Framework which meet the confidentiality, consistency and appropriate use conditions and with which Egypt has an international exchange of information agreement in effect that allows for the automatic exchange of tax information remains in place. This recommendation remains in place since the 2017/2018 peer review.

It is recommended that Egypt take steps to implement processes or written procedures to ensure that the exchange of information is conducted in a manner consistent with the terms of reference relating to the exchange of information framework ahead of its first exchanges of information. This recommendation remains in place since the 2018/2019 peer review.

Appropriate use of CbC reports

Egypt does not yet have controls in place to ensure the appropriate use of CbC reports.

It is recommended that Egypt take steps to ensure that the appropriate use condition is met ahead of the first exchanges of information. This recommendation remains in place since the 2017/2018 peer review.

Estonia

Overview of CbC reporting requirements

First reporting fiscal year: Commencing on or after 1 January 2016

Consolidated group revenue threshold: EUR 750 million

Filing deadline: 12 months following the end of the reporting fiscal year

Local filing required: Yes, for reporting fiscal years commencing on or after 1 January 2017

Surrogate parent entity filing permitted: Yes

First review of the domestic legal framework: 2017/2018

Summary of recommendations

Area of implementation	Recommendations for improvement
Domestic legal and administrative framework	None.
Exchange of information framework	None.
Appropriate use	None.

The domestic legal and administrative framework

Estonia confirms that its rules have not changed and continue to be applied effectively. Estonia continues to meet all terms of reference.[1 2]

The exchange of information framework

Estonia confirms that its rules have not changed and continue to be applied effectively. Estonia continues to meet all terms of reference.

Appropriate use of CbC reports

Estonia confirms that its rules have not changed and continue to be applied effectively. Estonia continues to meet all terms of reference.

Notes

[1] Estonia's 2017/2018 peer review included a monitoring point relating to the threshold calculation rule which would be applied in a manner consistent with the OECD guidance on currency fluctuations (paragraph 8 (a) ii. of the terms of reference). This monitoring point remains in place.

[2] Estonia's 2017/2018 peer review included a general monitoring point relating to a specific process to that would allow to take appropriate measures in case Estonia is notified by another jurisdiction that such other jurisdiction has reason to believe that an error may have led to incorrect or incomplete information reporting by a Reporting Entity or that there is non-compliance of a Reporting Entity with respect to its obligation to file a CbC report. This monitoring point remains in place.

Eswatini (Kingdom of)

Overview of CbC reporting requirements

The Kingdom of Eswatini (Eswatini) has not yet introduced a requirement for the filing of CbC reports, as required under the BEPS Action 13 (CbC reporting) minimum standard.

Summary of recommendations

Area of implementation	Recommendations for improvement
Domestic legal and administrative framework	It is recommended that Eswatini take steps to implement a domestic legal and administrative framework to impose and enforce CbC reporting requirements as soon as possible.
Exchange of information framework	It is recommended that Eswatini take steps to have qualifying competent authority agreements in effect with jurisdictions of the Inclusive Framework that meet the confidentiality, consistency and appropriate use conditions and with which Eswatini has an international exchange of information agreement in effect that allows for the automatic exchange of tax information. It is recommended that Eswatini take steps to implement the necessary processes or written procedures to ensure that the exchange of information is conducted in a manner consistent with the terms of reference relating to the exchange of information framework.
Appropriate use	It is recommended that Eswatini take steps to ensure that the appropriate use condition is met ahead of the first exchanges of information.

The domestic legal and administrative framework

Eswatini does not yet have legislation in place to implement the BEPS Action 13 minimum standard.

It is recommended that Eswatini take steps to implement a domestic legal and administrative framework to impose and enforce CbC reporting requirements as soon as possible. This recommendation remains in place since the 2019/2020 peer review.

The exchange of information framework

Eswatini has no bilateral relationships in place for the exchange of CbC reports nor processes to ensure that the exchange of information is conducted in a manner consistent with the terms of reference relating to the exchange of information framework.

It is recommended that Eswatini take steps to have qualifying competent authority agreements in effect with jurisdictions of the Inclusive Framework that meet the confidentiality, consistency and appropriate use conditions and with which Eswatini has an international exchange of information agreement in effect that allows for the automatic exchange of tax information. This recommendation remains in place since the 2019/2020 peer review.

It is recommended that Eswatini take steps to implement the necessary processes or written procedures to ensure that the exchange of information is conducted in a manner consistent with the terms of reference relating to the exchange of information framework. This recommendation remains in place since the 2019/2020 peer review.

Appropriate use of CbC reports

Eswatini does not yet have controls in place to ensure the appropriate use of CbC reports.

It is recommended that Eswatini take steps to ensure that the appropriate use condition is met ahead of the first exchanges of information. This recommendation remains in place since the 2019/2020 peer review.

Faroe Islands

Overview of CbC reporting requirements

First reporting fiscal year: Commencing on or after 20 December 2019

Consolidated group revenue threshold: DKK 5.6 billion

Filing deadline: 12 months following the end of the reporting fiscal year

Local filing required: Yes

Surrogate parent entity filing permitted: Yes

First review of the domestic legal framework: 2019/2020

Summary of recommendations

Area of implementation	Recommendations for improvement
Domestic legal and administrative framework	It is recommended that the Faroe Islands take steps to implement procedures to ensure effective implementation of the filing requirement. It is recommended that the Faroe Islands take steps to ensure that local filing only occurs in the circumstances permitted under the minimum standard.
Exchange of information framework	It is recommended that the Faroe Islands take steps to implement processes or written procedures to ensure that the exchange of information is conducted in a manner consistent with the terms of reference relating to the exchange of information framework.
Appropriate use	It is recommended that the Faroe Islands take steps to ensure that the appropriate use condition is met ahead of the first exchanges of information.

The domestic legal and administrative framework

The Faroe Islands' 2019/2020 peer review recommended that the Faroe Islands take steps to amend legislation or otherwise clarify that an MNE Group should consider its requirement to file using the consolidated group revenue of its fiscal year immediately preceding a reporting fiscal year for comparison with the threshold. The Faroe Islands has amended its legislation and this recommendation is removed.[1]

The Faroe Islands' 2019/2020 peer review recommended that the Faroe Islands take steps to amend legislation or otherwise clarify that there are no exemptions from the filing requirement for MNE Groups who meet the threshold requirement in the Faroe Islands. The Faroe Islands has amended its legislation and this recommendation is removed.[2]

The Faroe Islands' 2019/2020 peer review recommended that the Faroe Islands take steps to amend legislation or otherwise clarify that a CbC report should be filed within 12 months of the end of the reporting period the report applies to. The Faroe Islands has clarified that this is an issue of translation and that the CbC report should be filed within 12 months of the end of the reporting period the report applies to, and this recommendation is removed.

It is recommended that the Faroe Islands take steps to implement procedures to ensure effective implementation of the filing requirement. This recommendation remains in place since the 2019/2020 peer review.

The Faroe Islands has a legislative requirement for local filing which is in effect despite the Faroe Islands not yet meeting all of the consistency, confidentiality and appropriate use conditions. It is therefore recommended that the Faroe Islands take steps to ensure that local filing only occurs in the circumstances permitted under the minimum standard. This recommendation remains in place since the 2022/2023 peer review.

The exchange of information framework

It is recommended that the Faroe Islands take steps to implement processes or written procedures to ensure that the exchange of information is conducted in a manner consistent with the terms of reference relating to the exchange of information framework. This recommendation remains in place since the 2019/2020 peer review.

Appropriate use of CbC reports

The Faroe Islands does not yet have controls in place to ensure the appropriate use of CbC reports.

It is recommended that the Faroe Islands take steps to ensure that the appropriate use condition is met ahead of the first exchanges of information. This recommendation remains in place since the 2019/2020 peer review.

Notes

[1] https://logir.fo/Logtingslog/39-fra-16-05-2024-um-broyting-i-logtingslog-um-landsskatt-og-kommunuskatt-Skattalogin

[2] Ibid.

Finland

Overview of CbC reporting requirements

First reporting fiscal year: Commencing on or after 1 January 2016

Consolidated group revenue threshold: EUR 750 million

Filing deadline: 12 months following the end of the reporting fiscal year

Local filing required: Yes

Surrogate parent entity filing permitted: Yes

First review of the domestic legal framework: 2017/2018

Summary of recommendations

Area of implementation	Recommendations for improvement
Domestic legal and administrative framework	None.
Exchange of information framework	None.
Appropriate use	None.

The domestic legal and administrative framework

Finland confirms that its rules have not changed and continue to be applied effectively. Finland continues to meet all terms of reference.

The exchange of information framework

Finland confirms that its rules have not changed and continue to be applied effectively. Finland continues to meet all terms of reference.

Appropriate use of CbC reports

Finland confirms that its rules have not changed and continue to be applied effectively. Finland continues to meet all terms of reference.

France

Overview of CbC reporting requirements

First reporting fiscal year: Commencing on or after 1 January 2016

Consolidated group revenue threshold: EUR 750 million

Filing deadline: 12 months following the end of the reporting fiscal year

Local filing required: Yes

Surrogate parent entity filing permitted: Yes

First review of the domestic legal framework: 2017/2018

Summary of recommendations

Area of implementation	Recommendations for improvement
Domestic legal and administrative framework	It is recommended that France ensure that local filing only occurs in the circumstances contained in the terms of reference.
Exchange of information framework	None.
Appropriate use	None.

The domestic legal and administrative framework

It is recommended that France ensure that local filing only occurs in the circumstances contained in the terms of reference. This recommendation remains in place since the 2017/2018 peer review.[1]

The exchange of information framework

France confirms that its rules have not changed and continue to be applied effectively. France continues to meet all terms of reference.[2]

Appropriate use of CbC reports

France confirms that its rules have not changed and continue to be applied effectively. France continues to meet all terms of reference.

Notes

[1] France's 2017/2018 peer review included a monitoring point with respect to the limitation of local filing to the instances of "Systemic Failure" as defined in paragraph 21 of the terms of reference. France confirms

that its legislation implies that the obligations under the CbC MCAA are complied with (in particular the obligation for a prior consultation between Competent Authorities under Section 6 of the CbC MCAA) and will only apply local filing if there is a "Systemic Failure". This monitoring point remains in place.

[2] France's 2021/2022 peer review included a monitoring point with respect to missing or incomplete information in CbC reports sent to another jurisdiction. France has since introduced changes to its IT systems to ensure such missing or incomplete information will be identifiable in advance, and these changes will be effective for future filing periods. This monitoring point remains in place.

Gabon

Overview of CbC reporting requirements

First reporting fiscal year: Commencing on or after 1 January 2017

Consolidated group revenue threshold: XAF 491 967 750 000

Filing deadline: 12 months following the end of the reporting fiscal year

Local filing required: Yes

Surrogate parent entity filing permitted: Yes

First review of the domestic legal framework: 2017/2018

Summary of recommendations

Area of implementation	Recommendations for improvement
Domestic legal and administrative framework	It is recommended that Gabon finalise its requirements, in particular to: • complete or introduce the definitions of "Constituent Entity", "Group" and "MNE Group" which appear to be incomplete or missing, and • define the requirements on the content of a CbC report. It is recommended that Gabon take steps to ensure that local filing only occurs in the circumstances permitted under the minimum standard. It is recommended that Gabon clarify that the annual consolidated group revenue threshold calculation rule applies in line with the OECD guidance on currency fluctuations in respect of an MNE Group whose Ultimate Parent Entity is located in a jurisdiction other than Gabon.
Exchange of information framework	It is recommended that Gabon take steps to have qualifying competent authority agreements in effect with jurisdictions of the Inclusive Framework that meet the confidentiality, consistency and appropriate use conditions and with which Gabon has an international exchange of information agreement in effect that allows for the automatic exchange of tax information. It is recommended that Gabon take steps to implement the necessary processes or written procedures to ensure that the exchange of information is conducted in a manner consistent with the terms of reference relating to the exchange of information framework.
Appropriate use	It is recommended that Gabon take steps to ensure that the appropriate use condition is met ahead of the first exchanges of information.

The domestic legal and administrative framework

It is recommended that Gabon finalise its requirements particularly to:

complete or introduce the definitions of "Constituent Entity", "Group" and "MNE Group" which appear to be incomplete or missing, and

define the requirements on the content of a CbC report.

This recommendation remains in place since the 2017/2018 peer review.

Gabon has a legislative requirement for local filing which is in effect despite Gabon not yet meeting all of the consistency, confidentiality and appropriate use conditions. It is therefore recommended that Gabon take steps to ensure that local filing only occurs in the circumstances permitted under the minimum standard.

Where the MNE Group draws up, or would draw up, its Consolidated Financial Statements in a currency other than that specified by Gabon, the reference to Gabon's threshold has the effect as if it were a reference to the equivalent in that currency at the average exchange rate for the accounting period. While this provision would not create an issue for MNE Groups whose Ultimate Parent Entity is a tax resident in Gabon, it may be incompatible with the guidance on currency fluctuations for MNE Groups whose Ultimate Parent Entity is located in another jurisdiction, if local filing requirements were applied in respect of a Constituent Entity (which is a Gabon tax resident) of an MNE Group which does not reach the threshold as determined in the jurisdiction of the Ultimate Parent Entity of such a Group.

This is an unintended consequence of having a local filing requirement and it is therefore recommended that Gabon clarify that the annual consolidated group revenue threshold calculation rule applies in line with the OECD guidance on currency fluctuations in respect of an MNE Group whose Ultimate Parent Entity is located in a jurisdiction other than Gabon.

The exchange of information framework

Gabon has no bilateral relationships in place for the exchange of CbC reports nor processes to ensure that the exchange of information is conducted in a manner consistent with the terms of reference relating to the exchange of information framework.

It is recommended that Gabon take steps to have qualifying competent authority agreements in effect with jurisdictions of the Inclusive Framework that meet the confidentiality, consistency and appropriate use conditions and with which Gabon has an international exchange of information agreement in effect that allows for the automatic exchange of tax information. This recommendation remains in place since the 2017/2018 peer review.

It is recommended that Gabon take steps to implement the necessary processes or written procedures to ensure that the exchange of information is conducted in a manner consistent with the terms of reference relating to the exchange of information framework. This recommendation remains in place since the 2018/2019 peer review.

Appropriate use of CbC reports

Gabon does not yet have controls in place to ensure the appropriate use of CbC reports.

It is recommended that Gabon take steps to ensure that the appropriate use condition is met ahead of the first exchanges of information. This recommendation remains in place since the 2017/2018 peer review.

Georgia

Overview of CbC reporting requirements

First reporting fiscal year: Commencing on or after 1 January 2025

Consolidated group revenue threshold: EUR 750 million

Filing deadline: before 31 December in the year following the accounting year

Local filing required: Yes

Surrogate parent entity filing permitted: Yes

First review of the domestic legal framework: 2021/2022

Summary of recommendations

Area of implementation	Recommendations for improvement
Domestic legal and administrative framework	It is recommended that Georgia take steps to amend legislation or otherwise ensure that the filing deadline is not more than 12 months from the end of the reporting fiscal year.
Exchange of information framework	It is recommended that Georgia take steps to have qualifying competent authority agreements in effect with jurisdictions of the Inclusive Framework that meet the confidentiality, consistency and appropriate use conditions and with which Georgia has an international exchange of information agreement in effect that allows for the automatic exchange of tax information.
Appropriate use	None.

The domestic legal and administrative framework

Georgia's 2021/2022 peer review included a recommendation that Georgia amend the legislation to include the definition of a Group in line with the standard. Georgia has amended the definition and this recommendation is therefore removed.[1]

Georgia's 2021/2022 peer review included a recommendation that Georgia publish the full content and format requirements of the CbC Report. Georgia has published the full content and format requirements of the CbC Report and this recommendation is therefore removed.[2]

Georgia's 2021/2022 peer review included a recommendation that Georgia amend the legislation to include an effective date for the requirement to file CbC reports. Georgia has introduced an effective date and this recommendation is therefore removed.[3]

Georgia has introduced a local filing requirement as part of the domestic CbC Reporting legislation.[4]

It is recommended that Georgia take steps to amend legislation or otherwise ensure that the filing deadline is not more than 12 months from the end of the reporting fiscal year. This recommendation remains in place since the 2021/2022 peer review.

The exchange of information framework

Georgia has no bilateral relationships in place for the exchange of CbC reports nor processes to ensure that the exchange of information is conducted in a manner consistent with the terms of reference relating to the exchange of information framework.

It is recommended that Georgia take steps to have qualifying competent authority agreements in effect with jurisdictions of the Inclusive Framework that meet the confidentiality, consistency and appropriate use conditions and with which Georgia has an international exchange of information agreement in effect that allows for the automatic exchange of tax information. This recommendation remains in place since the 2017/2018 peer review.

Georgia's 2017/2018 peer review included a recommendation that Georgia take steps to implement the necessary processes or written procedures to ensure that the exchange of information is conducted in a manner consistent with the terms of reference relating to the exchange of information framework. These processes are in place and the recommendation is now removed.

Appropriate use of CbC reports

Georgia's 2017/2018 peer review included a recommendation that Georgia take steps to ensure that the appropriate use condition is met ahead of the first exchanges of information. Georgia now has controls in place to ensure the appropriate use of CbC reports and the recommendation is removed.

Georgia meets all terms of reference with respect to the appropriate use condition.

Notes

[1] https://matsne.gov.ge/ka/document/view/6187508?publication=0.

[2] Ibid.

[3] Ibid.

[4] Ibid.

Germany

Overview of CbC reporting requirements

First reporting fiscal year: Commencing on or after 1 January 2016

Consolidated group revenue threshold: EUR 750 million

Filing deadline: 12 months following the end of the reporting fiscal year

Local filing required: Yes, for reporting fiscal years commencing on or after 1 January 2017

Surrogate parent entity filing permitted: Yes

First review of the domestic legal framework: 2017/2018

Summary of recommendations

Area of implementation	Recommendations for improvement
Domestic legal and administrative framework	None.
Exchange of information framework	None.
Appropriate use	None.

The domestic legal and administrative framework

Germany confirms that its rules have not changed and continue to be applied effectively. Germany continues to meet all terms of reference.

The exchange of information framework

Germany's 2022/2023 peer report included a monitoring point that Germany introduce changes to ensure incorrect information in CbC reports did not cause those reports to be rejected by another jurisdiction. Germany has since introduced changes to its IT systems to address this issue, and this monitoring point is therefore removed.

Germany confirms that its rules have not changed and continue to be applied effectively. Germany continues to meet all terms of reference.

Appropriate use of CbC reports

Germany confirms that its rules have not changed and continue to be applied effectively. Germany continues to meet all terms of reference.

Gibraltar

Overview of CbC reporting requirements

First reporting fiscal year: Commencing on or after 1 January 2016

Consolidated group revenue threshold: EUR 750 million

Filing deadline: 12 months following the end of the reporting fiscal year

Local filing required: Yes, for reporting fiscal years commencing on or after 1 January 2017

Surrogate parent entity filing permitted: Yes

First review of the domestic legal framework: 2019/2020

Summary of recommendations

Area of implementation	Recommendations for improvement
Domestic legal and administrative framework	None.
Exchange of information framework	None.
Appropriate use	None.

The domestic legal and administrative framework

Gibraltar confirms that its rules have not changed and continue to be applied effectively. Gibraltar continues to meet all terms of reference.

The exchange of information framework

Gibraltar confirms that its rules have not changed and continue to be applied effectively. Gibraltar continues to meet all terms of reference.

Appropriate use of CbC reports

Gibraltar confirms that its rules have not changed and continue to be applied effectively. Gibraltar continues to meet all terms of reference.

Greece

Overview of CbC reporting requirements

First reporting fiscal year: Commencing on or after 1 January 2016

Consolidated group revenue threshold: EUR 750 million

Filing deadline: 12 months following the end of the reporting fiscal year

Local filing required: Yes

Surrogate parent entity filing permitted: Yes

First review of the domestic legal framework: 2017/2018

Summary of recommendations

Area of implementation	Recommendations for improvement
Domestic legal and administrative framework	None.
Exchange of information framework	None.
Appropriate use	None.

The domestic legal and administrative framework

Greece confirms that its rules have not changed and continue to be applied effectively. Greece continues to meet all terms of reference.[1]

The exchange of information framework

Greece confirms that its rules have not changed and continue to be applied effectively. Greece continues to meet all terms of reference.[2]

Appropriate use of CbC reports

Greece confirms that its rules have not changed and continue to be applied effectively. Greece continues to meet all terms of reference.

Notes

[1] Greece's 2017/2018 peer review included a general monitoring point relating to a specific process to that would allow to take appropriate measures in case Greece is notified by another jurisdiction that such other

jurisdiction has reason to believe that an error may have led to incorrect or incomplete information reporting by a Reporting Entity or that there is non-compliance of a Reporting Entity with respect to its obligation to file a CbC report. This monitoring point remains in place.

[2] Greece's 2021/2022 peer review included a monitoring point with respect to missing or incomplete information in CbC reports sent to another jurisdiction. Greece has since introduced changes to its IT systems to ensure such missing or incomplete information will be identifiable in advance, and these changes will be effective for future filing periods. This monitoring point remains in place.

Greenland

Overview of CbC reporting requirements

First reporting fiscal year: Commencing on or after 1 January 2019

Consolidated group revenue threshold: DKK 5.6 billion

Filing deadline: 12 months following the end of the reporting fiscal year

Local filing required: Yes

Surrogate parent entity filing permitted: Yes

First review of the domestic legal framework: 2019/2020

Summary of recommendations

Area of implementation	Recommendations for improvement
Domestic legal and administrative framework	It is recommended that Greenland clarify that the annual consolidated group revenue threshold calculation rule applies in line with the OECD guidance on currency fluctuations in respect of an MNE Group whose Ultimate Parent Entity is located in a jurisdiction other than Greenland.
Exchange of information framework	It is recommended that Greenland take steps to have qualifying competent authority agreements in effect with jurisdictions of the Inclusive Framework which meet the confidentiality, consistency and appropriate use conditions and with which Greenland has an international exchange of information agreement in effect that allows for the automatic exchange of tax information. It is recommended that Greenland take steps to implement processes or written procedures to ensure that the exchange of information is conducted in a manner consistent with the terms of reference relating to the exchange of information framework.
Appropriate use	None.

The domestic legal and administrative framework

It is recommended that Greenland clarify that the annual consolidated group revenue threshold calculation rule applies in line with the OECD guidance on currency fluctuations in respect of an MNE Group whose Ultimate Parent Entity is located in a jurisdiction other than Greenland. This recommendation remains in place since the 2019/2020 peer review.

The exchange of information framework

Greenland has no bilateral relationships in place for the exchange of CbC reports nor processes to ensure that the exchange of information is conducted in a manner consistent with the terms of reference relating to the exchange of information framework.

It is recommended that Greenland take steps to have Qualifying Competent Authority Agreements (QCAAs) in effect with jurisdictions of the Inclusive Framework which meet the confidentiality, consistency and appropriate use conditions and with which Greenland has an international exchange of information agreement in effect that allows for the automatic exchange of tax information. This recommendation remains in place since the 2019/2020 peer review.

It is recommended that Greenland take steps to implement processes or written procedures to ensure that the exchange of information is conducted in a manner consistent with the terms of reference relating to the exchange of information framework. This recommendation remains in place since the 2019/2020 peer review.

Appropriate use of CbC reports

Greenland confirms that its rules have not changed and continue to be applied effectively. Greenland continues to meet all terms of reference.

Grenada

Overview of CbC reporting requirements

Grenada has not yet introduced a requirement for the filing of CbC reports, as required under the BEPS Action 13 (CbC reporting) minimum standard.

Summary of recommendations

Area of implementation	Recommendations for improvement
Domestic legal and administrative framework	It is recommended that Grenada take steps to implement a domestic legal and administrative framework to impose and enforce CbC reporting requirements as soon as possible.
Exchange of information framework	It is recommended that Grenada take steps to have qualifying competent authority agreements in effect with jurisdictions of the Inclusive Framework that meet the confidentiality, consistency and appropriate use conditions and with which Grenada has an international exchange of information agreement in effect that allows for the automatic exchange of tax information. It is recommended that Grenada take steps to implement the necessary processes or written procedures to ensure that the exchange of information is conducted in a manner consistent with the terms of reference relating to the exchange of information framework.
Appropriate use	It is recommended that Grenada take steps to ensure that the appropriate use condition is met ahead of the first exchanges of information.

The domestic legal and administrative framework

Grenada does not yet have legislation in place to implement the BEPS Action 13 minimum standard.

It is recommended that Grenada take steps to implement a domestic legal and administrative framework to impose and enforce CbC reporting requirements as soon as possible. This recommendation remains in place since the 2019/2020 peer review.

The exchange of information framework

Grenada has no bilateral relationships in place for the exchange of CbC reports nor processes to ensure that the exchange of information is conducted in a manner consistent with the terms of reference relating to the exchange of information framework.

It is recommended that Grenada take steps to have qualifying competent authority agreements in effect with jurisdictions of the Inclusive Framework that meet the confidentiality, consistency and appropriate use conditions and with which Grenada has an international exchange of information agreement in effect that allows for the automatic exchange of tax information. This recommendation remains in place since the 2019/2020 peer review.

It is recommended that Grenada take steps to implement the necessary processes or written procedures to ensure that the exchange of information is conducted in a manner consistent with the terms of reference relating to the exchange of information framework. This recommendation remains in place since the 2019/2020 peer review.

Appropriate use of CbC reports

Grenada does not yet have controls in place to ensure the appropriate use of CbC reports.

It is recommended that Grenada take steps to ensure that the appropriate use condition is met ahead of the first exchanges of information. This recommendation remains in place since the 2019/2020 peer review.

Guernsey

Overview of CbC reporting requirements

First reporting fiscal year: Commencing on or after 1 January 2016

Consolidated group revenue threshold: EUR 750 million

Filing deadline: 12 months following the end of the reporting fiscal year

Local filing required: Yes

Surrogate parent entity filing permitted: Yes

First review of the domestic legal framework: 2017/2018

Summary of recommendations

Area of implementation	Recommendations for improvement
Domestic legal and administrative framework	None.
Exchange of information framework	None.
Appropriate use	None.

The domestic legal and administrative framework

Guernsey confirms that its rules have not changed and continue to be applied effectively. Guernsey continues to meet all terms of reference.

The exchange of information framework

Guernsey made some exchanges of CbC reports after the deadline. This was caused by an issue which has since been resolved and so no recommendation is required.

Guernsey confirms that its rules have not changed and continue to be applied effectively. Guernsey continues to meet all terms of reference.

Appropriate use of CbC reports

Guernsey confirms that its rules have not changed and continue to be applied effectively. Guernsey continues to meet all terms of reference.

Haiti

Overview of CbC reporting requirements

Haiti has not yet introduced a requirement for the filing of CbC reports, as required under the BEPS Action 13 (CbC reporting) minimum standard.

Summary of recommendations

Area of implementation	Recommendations for improvement
Domestic legal and administrative framework	It is recommended that Haiti take steps to implement a domestic legal and administrative framework to impose and enforce CbC reporting requirements as soon as possible.
Exchange of information framework	It is recommended that Haiti take steps to have qualifying competent authority agreements in effect with jurisdictions of the Inclusive Framework that meet the confidentiality, consistency and appropriate use conditions and with which Haiti has an international exchange of information agreement in effect that allows for the automatic exchange of tax information It is recommended that Haiti take steps to implement the necessary processes or written procedures to ensure that the exchange of information is conducted in a manner consistent with the terms of reference relating to the exchange of information framework.
Appropriate use	It is recommended that Haiti take steps to ensure that the appropriate use condition is met ahead of the first exchanges of information.

The domestic legal and administrative framework

Haiti does not yet have legislation in place to implement the BEPS Action 13 minimum standard.

It is recommended that Haiti take steps to implement a domestic legal and administrative framework to impose and enforce CbC reporting requirements as soon as possible. This recommendation remains in place since the 2017/2018 peer review.

The exchange of information framework

Haiti has no bilateral relationships in place for the exchange of CbC reports nor processes to ensure that the exchange of information is conducted in a manner consistent with the terms of reference relating to the exchange of information framework.

It is recommended that Haiti take steps to have qualifying competent authority agreements in effect with jurisdictions of the Inclusive Framework that meet the confidentiality, consistency and appropriate use conditions and with which Haiti has an international exchange of information agreement in effect that allows for the automatic exchange of tax information. This recommendation remains in place since the 2017/2018 peer review.

It is recommended that Haiti take steps to implement the necessary processes or written procedures to ensure that the exchange of information is conducted in a manner consistent with the terms of reference relating to the exchange of information framework. This recommendation remains in place since the 2018/2019 peer review.

Appropriate use of CbC reports

Haiti does not yet have controls in place to ensure the appropriate use of CbC reports.

It is recommended that Haiti take steps to ensure that the appropriate use condition is met ahead of the first exchanges of information. This recommendation remains in place since the 2017/2018 peer review.

Honduras

Overview of CbC reporting requirements

First reporting fiscal year: Commencing on or after 1 January 2025

Consolidated group revenue threshold: EUR 750 million or HNL 19 billion

Filing deadline: 12 months following the end of the reporting fiscal year

Local filing required: Yes

Surrogate parent entity filing permitted: Yes

First review of the domestic legal framework: 2023/2024

Summary of recommendations

Area of implementation	Recommendations for improvement
Domestic legal and administrative framework	It is recommended that Honduras take steps to ensure that local filing only occurs in the circumstances permitted under the minimum standard.
Exchange of information framework	It is recommended that Honduras take steps to have qualifying competent authority agreements in effect with jurisdictions of the Inclusive Framework that meet the confidentiality, consistency and appropriate use conditions and with which Honduras has an international exchange of information agreement in effect that allows for the automatic exchange of tax information. It is recommended that Honduras take steps to implement the necessary processes or written procedures to ensure that the exchange of information is conducted in a manner consistent with the terms of reference relating to the exchange of information framework.
Appropriate use	It is recommended that Honduras take steps to ensure that the appropriate use condition is met ahead of the first exchanges of information.

The domestic legal and administrative framework

Honduras's 2020/2021 peer review included a recommendation to take steps to implement a domestic legal and administrative framework to impose and enforce CbC reporting requirements as soon as possible. Honduras has now introduced a CbC reporting filing requirement which applies to all Ultimate Parent Entities of MNE Groups above a certain threshold and which requires inclusion of all constituent entities. [1]

A CbC reporting filing obligation applies in Honduras for fiscal years commencing on or after 1 January 2025 and filing is required 12 months after the reporting year end. Honduras has enforcement requirements to ensure compliance with rules on CbC reporting.

Honduras has a legislative requirement for local filing which is in effect despite Honduras not yet meeting all of the consistency, confidentiality and appropriate use conditions. It is therefore recommended that Honduras take steps to ensure that local filing only occurs in the circumstances permitted under the minimum standard.

The exchange of information framework

Honduras has no bilateral relationships in place for the exchange of CbC reports nor processes to ensure that the exchange of information is conducted in a manner consistent with the terms of reference relating to the exchange of information framework.

It is recommended that Honduras take steps to have qualifying competent authority agreements in effect with jurisdictions of the Inclusive Framework that meet the confidentiality, consistency and appropriate use conditions and with which Honduras has an international exchange of information agreement in effect that allows for the automatic exchange of tax information. This recommendation remains in place since the 2020/2021 peer review.

It is recommended that Honduras take steps to implement the necessary processes or written procedures to ensure that the exchange of information is conducted in a manner consistent with the terms of reference relating to the exchange of information framework. This recommendation remains in place since the 2020/2021 peer review.

Appropriate use of CbC reports

Honduras does not yet have controls in place to ensure the appropriate use of CbC reports.

It is recommended that Honduras take steps to ensure that the appropriate use condition is met ahead of the first exchanges of information. This recommendation remains in place since the 2020/2021 peer review.

Notes

[1] https://juntec.org.hn/wp-content/uploads/2024/04/GACETA-19-DE-MARZO-DE-2024-36489-SECCION-A.pdf

Hong Kong (China)

Overview of CbC reporting requirements

First reporting fiscal year: Commencing on or after 1 January 2018. Hong Kong also allowed MNE Groups to file a CbC report on a voluntary basis, for reporting fiscal years commencing between 1 January 2016 and 31 December 2017.

Consolidated group revenue threshold: HKD 6.8 billion

Filing deadline: 12 months following the end of the reporting fiscal year

Local filing required: Yes

Surrogate parent entity filing permitted: Yes

First review of the domestic legal framework: 2018/2019

Summary of recommendations

Area of implementation	Recommendations for improvement
Domestic legal and administrative framework	None.
Exchange of information framework	None.
Appropriate use	None.

The domestic legal and administrative framework

Hong Kong confirms that its rules have not changed and continue to be applied effectively. Hong Kong continues to meet all terms of reference.

The exchange of information framework

Hong Kong confirms that its rules have not changed and continue to be applied effectively. Hong Kong continues to meet all terms of reference.

Appropriate use of CbC reports

Hong Kong confirms that its rules have not changed and continue to be applied effectively. Hong Kong continues to meet all terms of reference.

Hungary

Overview of CbC reporting requirements

First reporting fiscal year: Commencing on or after 1 January 2016

Consolidated group revenue threshold: EUR 750 million

Filing deadline: 12 months following the end of the reporting fiscal year

Local filing required: Yes, for reporting fiscal years commencing on or after 1 January 2017

Surrogate parent entity filing permitted: Yes

First review of the domestic legal framework: 2017/2018

Summary of recommendations

Area of implementation	Recommendations for improvement
Domestic legal and administrative framework	None.
Exchange of information framework	None.
Appropriate use	None.

The domestic legal and administrative framework

Hungary confirms that its rules have not changed and continue to be applied effectively. Hungary continues to meet all terms of reference.

The exchange of information framework

Hungary confirms that its rules have not changed and continue to be applied effectively. Hungary continues to meet all terms of reference.

Appropriate use of CbC reports

Hungary confirms that its rules have not changed and continue to be applied effectively. Hungary continues to meet all terms of reference.

Iceland

Overview of CbC reporting requirements

First reporting fiscal year: Commencing on or after 1 January 2017

Consolidated group revenue threshold: ISK 100 billion

Filing deadline: 12 months following the end of the reporting fiscal year

Local filing required: Yes

Surrogate parent entity filing permitted: Yes

First review of the domestic legal framework: 2017/2018

Summary of recommendations

Area of implementation	Recommendations for improvement
Domestic legal and administrative framework	None.
Exchange of information framework	None.
Appropriate use	None.

The domestic legal and administrative framework

Iceland confirms that its rules have not changed and continue to be applied effectively. Iceland continues to meet all terms of reference.[1]

The exchange of information framework

Iceland made some exchanges of CbC reports after the deadline. This was caused by a technical issue which has since been resolved and so no recommendation is required.

Iceland confirms that its rules have not changed and continue to be applied effectively. Iceland continues to meet all terms of reference.

Appropriate use of CbC reports

Iceland confirms that its rules have not changed and continue to be applied effectively. Iceland continues to meet all terms of reference.

Note

[1] Iceland's 2017/2018 peer review included a general monitoring point relating to a specific process that would allow it to take appropriate measures in case Iceland is notified by another jurisdiction that such other jurisdiction has reason to believe that an error may have led to incorrect or incomplete information reporting by a Reporting Entity or that there is non-compliance of a Reporting Entity with respect to its obligation to file a CbC report. This monitoring point remains in place.

India

Overview of CbC reporting requirements

First reporting fiscal year: Commencing on or after 1 April 2016

Consolidated group revenue threshold: INR 64 billion

Filing deadline: 12 months following the end of the reporting fiscal year

Local filing required: Yes

Surrogate parent entity filing permitted: Yes

First review of the domestic legal framework: 2017/2018

Summary of recommendations

Area of implementation	Recommendations for improvement
Domestic legal and administrative framework	It is recommended that India amend or otherwise clarify that the annual consolidated group revenue threshold calculation rule applies in a manner consistent with the OECD guidance on currency fluctuations in respect of an MNE Group whose Ultimate Parent Entity is located in a jurisdiction other than India. It is recommended that India amend its legislation or otherwise takes steps to ensure that local filing is only required in the circumstances contained in the terms of reference.
Exchange of information framework	None.
Appropriate use	None.

The domestic legal and administrative framework

It is recommended that India amend or otherwise clarify that the annual consolidated group revenue threshold calculation rule applies in a manner consistent with the OECD guidance on currency fluctuations in respect of an MNE Group whose Ultimate Parent Entity is located in a jurisdiction other than India. This recommendation remains unchanged since the 2017/2018 peer review.

It is recommended that India amend its legislation or otherwise takes steps to ensure that local filing is only required in the circumstances contained in the terms of reference. This recommendation remains unchanged since the 2017/2018 peer review.

The exchange of information framework

India confirms that its rules have not changed and continue to be applied effectively. India continues to meet all terms of reference.

Appropriate use of CbC reports

India confirms that its rules have not changed and continue to be applied effectively. India continues to meet all terms of reference.

Indonesia

Overview of CbC reporting requirements

First reporting fiscal year: Commencing on or after 1 January 2016

Consolidated group revenue threshold: IDR 11 trillion

Filing deadline: 12 months following the end of the reporting fiscal year

Local filing required: Yes

Surrogate parent entity filing permitted: Yes

First review of the domestic legal framework: 2017/2018

Summary of recommendations

Area of implementation	Recommendations for improvement
Domestic legal and administrative framework	None.
Exchange of information framework	None.
Appropriate use	None.

The domestic legal and administrative framework

Indonesia confirms that its rules have not changed and continue to be applied effectively. Indonesia continues to meet all terms of reference.[1] [2]

The exchange of information framework

Indonesia confirms that its rules have not changed and continue to be applied effectively. Indonesia continues to meet all terms of reference.

Appropriate use of CbC reports

Indonesia confirms that its rules have not changed and continue to be applied effectively. Indonesia continues to meet all terms of reference.

Notes

[1] Indonesia's 2017/2018 peer review included a monitoring point in relation to the local filing in case of "systemic failure". This monitoring point remains in place.

[2] Indonesia's 2017/2018 peer review included a monitoring point in relation to one of the conditions to deactivate the local filing obligation in case of surrogate filing. This monitoring point remains in place.

Ireland

Overview of CbC reporting requirements

First reporting fiscal year: Commencing on or after 1 January 2016

Consolidated group revenue threshold: EUR 750 million

Filing deadline: 12 months following the end of the reporting fiscal year

Local filing required: Yes

Surrogate parent entity filing permitted: Yes

First review of the domestic legal framework: 2017/2018

Summary of recommendations

Area of implementation	Recommendations for improvement
Domestic legal and administrative framework	None.
Exchange of information framework	None.
Appropriate use	None.

The domestic legal and administrative framework

Ireland confirms that its rules have not changed and continue to be applied effectively. Ireland continues to meet all terms of reference.[1]

The exchange of information framework

Ireland confirms that its rules have not changed and continue to be applied effectively. Ireland continues to meet all terms of reference.

Appropriate use of CbC reports

Ireland confirms that its rules have not changed and continue to be applied effectively. Ireland continues to meet all terms of reference.

Note

[1] Ireland's 2017/2018 peer review included a monitoring point relating to the conditions under which local filing may be required (paragraph 8 (c) iv. b) of the terms of reference). This monitoring point remains in place.

Isle of Man

Overview of CbC reporting requirements

First reporting fiscal year: Commencing on or after 1 January 2017. The Isle of Man also allowed MNE Groups to file a CbC report on a voluntary basis, for reporting fiscal years commencing between 1 January 2016 and 31 December 2016.

Consolidated group revenue threshold: EUR 750 million

Filing deadline: 12 months and one day following the end of the reporting fiscal year

Local filing required: Yes

Surrogate parent entity filing permitted: Yes

First review of the domestic legal framework: 2017/2018

Summary of recommendations

Area of implementation	Recommendations for improvement
Domestic legal and administrative framework	None.
Exchange of information framework	None.
Appropriate use	None.

The domestic legal and administrative framework

The Isle of Man confirms that its rules have not changed and continue to be applied effectively. The Isle of Man continues to meet all terms of reference.

The exchange of information framework

The Isle of Man confirms that its rules have not changed and continue to be applied effectively. The Isle of Man continues to meet all terms of reference.

Appropriate use of CbC reports

The Isle of Man confirms that its rules have not changed and continue to be applied effectively. The Isle of Man continues to meet all terms of reference.

Israel

Overview of CbC reporting requirements

First reporting fiscal year: Commencing on or after 1 January 2022. Israel also allowed MNE Groups to file a CbC report on a voluntary basis, for reporting fiscal years commencing between 1 January and 31 December 2021.

Consolidated group revenue threshold: NIS 3.4 billion

Filing deadline: 12 months following the end of the reporting fiscal year

Local filing required: Yes

Surrogate parent entity filing permitted: Yes

First review of the domestic legal framework: 2022/2023

Summary of recommendations

Area of implementation	Recommendations for improvement
Domestic legal and administrative framework	It is recommended that Israel amend or otherwise clarify the definition of "MNE Group", "Constituent Entity" and to include a definition of "Consolidated Financial Statements" that is in line with the standard. It is recommended that Israel amend its legislation or otherwise takes steps to ensure that local filing is only required in the circumstances contained in the terms of reference. It is recommended that Israel introduce rules providing that local filing will not apply for a Constituent Entity resident in Israel when the CbC report of the CbC Group to which it belongs has been filed by a Surrogate Parent Entity in its jurisdiction of tax residence. It is recommended that Israel take steps to ensure that enforcement provisions and monitoring relating to the enforcement of CbCR filing obligations are implemented.
Exchange of information framework	None.
Appropriate use	None.

The domestic legal and administrative framework

Israel has a number of recommendations to improve the legislation. These recommendations remain in place since the 2022/2023 peer review.[1] [2]

The definition of MNE Group

The definition in Israel's legislation refers to two or more related entities where at least one of them is a foreign resident. The definition of MNE Group should also include entities which are subject to tax in different jurisdictions through a permanent establishment and it does not seem to be the case in Israel.

It is recommended that Israel amend or otherwise clarify the definition of MNE Group to be in line with the standard.

The definition of Constituent Entity

Israel's legislation refers to the term "Entity", which is defined as "a body of persons, including a business unit of a group of persons for which separate financial statements are prepared". Israel's legislation defines "body or persons" as any "public body, incorporated or amalgamated, and any company, fraternity, fellowship or society, whether incorporated or not." This definition seems narrower than the term under BEPS Action 13, which is intended to cover all types of entities that would have been required to be included in the MNE Group Consolidated Financial Statements, permanent establishments and entities that would have been excluded from the Consolidated Financial Statements solely on size or materiality grounds.

It is recommended that Israel amend its legislation to include a definition of "Constituent Entity" that is in line with the standard.

The definition of Consolidated Financial Statements

Israel's legislation does not include a definition of "Consolidated Financial Statements".

It is recommended that Israel amend its legislation to include a definition of "Consolidated Financial Statements" that is in line with the standard.

The local filing provision

Israel's legislation provides that "The director will be entitled to oblige an entity in the multinational group..., which is a resident of Israel, to submit an ultimate parent entity report, even if it is not an entity required to report...". This provision may impose a local filing obligation to any constituent entity of a foreign MNE Group which is a resident of Israel, regardless of whether the MNE Group meets the revenue threshold to file a CbC report. It should be clarified that local filing only applies to entities in MNE Groups where the threshold for filing a CbC report is exceeded.

Local filing can be required in Israel if the "exchange of information between Israel and the country where the ultimate parent entity report was submitted was suspended contrary to the terms of the competent authority agreement, or no information was received, for some other reason, from that country, regarding multinational groups that include an entity in Israel." This provision may be interpreted in a broader meaning than the situation of a "Systemic Failure" under the term of reference. Under Israel's legislation, local filing may be required in circumstances where there is non-filing of a CbC report in a jurisdiction, which would not constitute a systemic failure to exchange.

It is recommended that Israel amend its legislation or otherwise takes steps to ensure that local filing is only required in the circumstances contained in the terms of reference.

Limitation on local filing in case of surrogate filing

Israel's legislation does not limit local filing in case of surrogate filing.

It is recommended that Israel take steps to amend its legislation or otherwise impose a limitation on local filing in case of surrogate filing in line with the standard.

Effective implementation

Israel's legislation includes a penalty in relation to the failure to comply with the obligation relating to CbC reports. It is however unclear whether this penalty would apply in cases of incorrect filing or incomplete filing of a CbC report. It is recommended that Israel take steps to ensure that enforcement provisions and monitoring relating to the enforcement of CbCR filing obligations are implemented.

The exchange of information framework

Israel confirms that its rules have not changed and continue to be applied effectively. Israel continues to meet all terms of reference.

Appropriate use of CbC reports

Israel confirms that its rules have not changed and continue to be applied effectively. Israel continues to meet all terms of reference.

Notes

[1] Israel's 2022/2023 peer review included a general monitoring point relating to a specific process that would allow Israel to take appropriate measures in case Israel is notified by another jurisdiction that such other jurisdiction has reason to believe that an error may have led to incorrect or incomplete information reporting by a Reporting Entity or that there is non-compliance of a Reporting Entity with respect to its obligation to file a CbC report. This monitoring point remains in place.

[2] Israel's 2022/2023 peer review included a monitoring point with respect to allowing, where local filing is required and there is more than one Constituent Entity of the same MNE Group that is resident for tax purposes in Israel, one Constituent Entity to be designated to file the CbC report which would satisfy the filing requirement of all the Constituent Entities of such MNE Group that are resident for tax purposes in Israel. This monitoring point remains in place.

Italy

Overview of CbC reporting requirements

First reporting fiscal year: Commencing on or after 1 January 2016

Consolidated group revenue threshold: EUR 750 million

Filing deadline: 12 months following the end of the reporting fiscal year

Local filing required: Yes

Surrogate parent entity filing permitted: Yes

First review of the domestic legal framework: 2017/2018

Summary of recommendations

Area of implementation	Recommendations for improvement
Domestic legal and administrative framework	None.
Exchange of information framework	None.
Appropriate use	None.

The domestic legal and administrative framework

Italy confirms that its rules have not changed and continue to be applied effectively. Italy continues to meet all terms of reference.

The exchange of information framework

Italy made some exchanges of CbC reports after the deadline. This was caused by a technical issue which has since been resolved and so no recommendation is required.

Italy confirms that its rules have not changed and continue to be applied effectively. Italy continues to meet all terms of reference.

Appropriate use of CbC reports

Italy confirms that its rules have not changed and continue to be applied effectively. Italy continues to meet all terms of reference.

Jamaica

Overview of CbC reporting requirements

Jamaica has not yet introduced a requirement for the filing of CbC reports, as required under the BEPS Action 13 (CbC reporting) minimum standard.

Summary of recommendations

Area of implementation	Recommendations for improvement
Domestic legal and administrative framework	It is recommended that Jamaica take steps to implement a domestic legal and administrative framework to impose and enforce CbC reporting requirements as soon as possible.
Exchange of information framework	It is recommended that Jamaica take steps to have qualifying competent authority agreements in effect with jurisdictions of the Inclusive Framework that meet the confidentiality, consistency and appropriate use conditions and with which Jamaica has an international exchange of information agreement in effect that allows for the automatic exchange of tax information. It is recommended that Jamaica take steps to implement the necessary processes or written procedures to ensure that the exchange of information is conducted in a manner consistent with the terms of reference relating to the exchange of information framework.
Appropriate use	It is recommended that Jamaica take steps to ensure that the appropriate use condition is met ahead of the first exchanges of information.

The domestic legal and administrative framework

Jamaica does not yet have legislation in place to implement the BEPS Action 13 minimum standard.

It is recommended that Jamaica take steps to implement a domestic legal and administrative framework to impose and enforce CbC reporting requirements as soon as possible. This recommendation remains in place since the 2018/2019 peer review.

The exchange of information framework

Jamaica has no bilateral relationships in place for the exchange of CbC reports nor processes to ensure that the exchange of information is conducted in a manner consistent with the terms of reference relating to the exchange of information framework.

It is recommended that Jamaica take steps to have qualifying competent authority agreements in effect with jurisdictions of the Inclusive Framework that meet the confidentiality, consistency and appropriate use conditions and with which Jamaica has an international exchange of information agreement in effect that allows for the automatic exchange of tax information. This recommendation remains in place since the 2018/2019 peer review.

It is recommended that Jamaica take steps to implement the necessary processes or written procedures to ensure that the exchange of information is conducted in a manner consistent with the terms of reference relating to the exchange of information framework. This recommendation remains in place since the 2018/2019 peer review.

Appropriate use of CbC reports

Jamaica does not yet have controls in place to ensure the appropriate use of CbC reports.

It is recommended that Jamaica take steps to ensure that the appropriate use condition is met ahead of the first exchanges of information. This recommendation remains in place since the 2018/2019 peer review.

Japan

Overview of CbC reporting requirements

First reporting fiscal year: Commencing on or after 1 April 2016. Japan also allowed MNE Groups to file a CbC report on a voluntary basis, for reporting fiscal years commencing between 1 January 2016 and 31 March 2016.

Consolidated group revenue threshold: JPY 100 billion

Filing deadline: 12 months following the end of the reporting fiscal year

Local filing required: Yes. Transitional relief from local filing requirements applied to the fiscal year 1 April 2016 to 31 March 2017, except for the case where local filing arose as a result of a Systemic Failure by another jurisdiction.

Surrogate parent entity filing permitted: Yes

First review of the domestic legal framework: 2017/2018

Summary of recommendations

Area of implementation	Recommendations for improvement
Domestic legal and administrative framework	None.
Exchange of information framework	None.
Appropriate use	None.

The domestic legal and administrative framework

Japan confirms that its rules have not changed and continue to be applied effectively. Japan continues to meet all terms of reference.

The exchange of information framework

Japan confirms that its rules have not changed and continue to be applied effectively. Japan continues to meet all terms of reference.

Appropriate use of CbC reports

Japan confirms that its rules have not changed and continue to be applied effectively. Japan continues to meet all terms of reference.

Jersey (Bailiwick of)

Overview of CbC reporting requirements

First reporting fiscal year: Commencing on or after 1 January 2016

Consolidated group revenue threshold: EUR 750 million

Filing deadline: 12 months following the end of the reporting fiscal year

Local filing required: Yes

Surrogate parent entity filing permitted: Yes

First review of the domestic legal framework: 2017/2018

Summary of recommendations

Area of implementation	Recommendations for improvement
Domestic legal and administrative framework	None.
Exchange of information framework	None.
Appropriate use	None.

The domestic legal and administrative framework

Jersey confirms that its rules have not changed and continue to be applied effectively. Jersey continues to meet all terms of reference.

The exchange of information framework

Jersey confirms that its rules have not changed and continue to be applied effectively. Jersey continues to meet all terms of reference.

Appropriate use of CbC reports

Jersey confirms that its rules have not changed and continue to be applied effectively. Jersey continues to meet all terms of reference.

Jordan

Overview of CbC reporting requirements

First reporting fiscal year: Beginning on or after 1 January 2021

Consolidated group revenue threshold: JOD 600 million

Filing deadline: Within 12 months following the end of the reporting fiscal year

Local filing required: Yes

Surrogate parent entity filing permitted: Yes

First review of domestic legal framework: 2021/2022

Summary of recommendations

Area of implementation	Recommendations for improvement
Domestic legal and administrative framework	It is recommended that Jordan amend legislation or otherwise ensure that requirements on the sources of data that can be used in completing the CbC report template are in line with the standard. It is recommended that Jordan take steps to amend legislation or otherwise ensure that the form and content required in the CbC Report is in line with the standard. It is recommended that Jordan introduce or complete the definitions of a "Group", "MNE Group", "Ultimate Parent Entity", "Constituent Entity", "Consolidated Financial Statements", "Fiscal Year", "Reporting Fiscal Year", "Reporting Entity", "Qualifying Competent Authority Agreement", "Surrogate Parent Entity", "Systemic Failure" and "International Agreement" in a manner that is consistent with the terms of reference. It is recommended that Jordan take steps to ensure that local filing only occurs in the circumstances permitted under the minimum standard. It is recommended that Jordan clarify the circumstances in which surrogate entity filing is permitted. It is recommended that Jordan clarify that the annual consolidated group revenue threshold calculation rule applies in line with the OECD guidance on currency fluctuations in respect of an MNE Group whose Ultimate Parent Entity is located in a jurisdiction other than Jordan.
Exchange of information framework	It is recommended that Jordan take steps to have qualifying competent authority agreements in effect with jurisdictions of the Inclusive Framework that meet the confidentiality, consistency and appropriate use conditions and with which Jordan has an international exchange of information agreement in effect that allows for the automatic exchange of tax information. It is recommended that Jordan take steps to implement the necessary processes or written procedures to ensure that the exchange of information is conducted in a manner consistent with the terms of reference relating to the exchange of information framework.
Appropriate use	It is recommended that Jordan take steps to ensure that the appropriate use condition is met ahead of the first exchanges of information.

The domestic legal and administrative framework

Jordan has the following recommendations relating to its domestic legal and administrative framework. These recommendations remain in place since the 2021/2022 peer review.

Timing of parent entity filing

Jordan's 2021/2022 peer review recommended that Jordan takes steps to amend legislation or otherwise clarify that the filing deadline is not more than 12 months from the end of the reporting fiscal year. Jordan has clarified that the filing deadline is not more than 12 months from the end of the reporting fiscal year and the recommendation is removed.

Use of audited consolidated financial statements as the source of data

Jordan's legislation specifies that the MNE Group must use audited consolidated financial statements in order to prepare the CbC report. Under the standard, an MNE Group may choose to use data from its consolidation reporting packages, from separate entity statutory financial statements, regulatory financial statements or internal management accounts and there is no requirement for financial statements to be audited. It is recommended that Jordan amend legislation or otherwise ensure that requirements on the sources of data that can be used in completing the CbC report template are in line with the standard.

Content of CbC Report

Jordan's legislation outlines the form and content of the CbC Report but requires more details in respect of income breakdown than is permitted under the standard. It is recommended that Jordan take steps to amend legislation or otherwise ensure that the form and content required in the CbC Report is in line with the standard.

The definition of Group

Jordan's legislation does not include a definition of "Group". It is recommended that Jordan amend its legislation to include a definition of "Group" that is in line with the standard.

The definition of MNE Group

The definition in Jordan's legislation refers to two or more related legal persons whose tax residence is in different countries, where those legal persons are considered a taxable person in their respective country of tax residence.

The definition of MNE Group should include businesses which are subject to tax in different jurisdictions through being taxable through a permanent establishment. It is recommended that Jordan amend the definition of MNE Group or otherwise clarify the definition to be in line with the standard.

The definition of Ultimate Parent Entity

The definition in Jordan's legislation refers to an entity that directly or indirectly owns stakes or shares in one or more multinational companies. The definition requires that the UPE is committed to preparing consolidated financial statements in accordance with international accounting standards generally accepted in the country in which it is tax resident.

The use of the term "committed" in Jordan's legislation, when referring to preparing consolidated financial statements, could be read as being optional. The definition in Jordan's legislation does not adequately capture the *requirement* to prepare consolidated financial statements, as is required under the standard.

Furthermore, the definition in Jordan's legislation also fails to cover circumstances where an entity owns directly or indirectly a sufficient interest in one or more other Constituent Entities such that it would required to prepare Consolidated Financial Statements if its equity interests were traded on a public securities exchange in its jurisdiction of tax residence (the "deemed listing provision"), which is required under the standard.

Finally, the definition in Jordan's legislation does not include the condition that no other Constituent Entity of the MNE Group owns directly or indirectly an interest described the first mentioned Constituent Entity.

It is recommended that Jordan amend the definition of UPE or otherwise clarify the definition to be in line with the standard.

The definition of Constituent Entity

Jordan's legislation does not include a definition of "Constituent Entity". It is recommended that Jordan amend its legislation to include a definition of "Constituent Entity" that is in line with the standard.

The definition of Consolidated Financial Statements

Jordan's legislation does not include a definition of "Consolidated Financial Statements". It is recommended that Jordan amend its legislation to include a definition of "Consolidated Financial Statements" that is in line with the standard.

The definition of Fiscal Year

Jordan's legislation does not include a definition of "Fiscal Year". It is recommended that Jordan amend its legislation to include a definition of "Fiscal Year" that is in line with the standard.

The definition of Reporting Fiscal Year

Jordan's legislation does not include a definition of "Reporting Fiscal Year". It is recommended that Jordan amend its legislation to include a definition of "Reporting Fiscal Year" that is in line with the standard.

The definition of Reporting Entity

The definition in Jordan's legislation refers to the taxpayer who submits the CbC report for each country to the relevant tax administration, on behalf of the MNE Group.

This definition does not outline who may be the Reporting Entity, for example the UPE, the Surrogate Parent Entity, or any other entity described in the legislation. Furthermore, it does not outline which entity is required to file the CbC report. It is recommended that Jordan amend the definition of Reporting Entity or otherwise clarify the definition to be in line with the standard.

The definition of Qualifying Competent Authority Agreement

Jordan's legislation does not include a definition of "Qualifying Competent Authority Agreement". It is recommended that Jordan amend its legislation to include a definition of "Qualifying Competent Authority Agreement" that is in line with the standard.

The definition of Surrogate Parent Entity

The definition in Jordan's legislation refers to the taxpayer affiliated with an MNE Group that is required to submit the CbC report to the department on behalf of the MNE Group.

The definition of Surrogate Parent Entity in the standard is intended to capture that the entity in question has been appointed by the MNE Group, as the sole substitute of the CbC Report, and only where certain conditions have been met (see below). It is recommended that Jordan amend the definition of Surrogate Parent Entity or otherwise clarify the definition to be in line with the standard.

The definition of Systemic Failure

Jordan's legislation does not include a definition of "Systemic Failure". It is recommended that Jordan amend its legislation to include a definition of "Systemic Failure" that is in line with the standard.

The definition of International Agreement

Jordan's legislation does not include a definition of "International Agreement". It is recommended that Jordan amend its legislation to include a definition of "International Agreement" that is in line with the standard.

The local filing provision

The local filing definition in Jordan's guidance applies to "a branch of this group in Jordan", meaning the MNE Group. The guidance does not include any further detail in respect of the circumstances under which local filing can take place. Furthermore, Jordan has a legislative requirement which is in effect despite Jordan not yet meeting all of the consistency, confidentiality and appropriate use conditions. It is therefore recommended that Jordan take steps to ensure that local filing only occurs in the circumstances permitted under the minimum standard.

Single entity filing

Jordan's 2021/2022 peer review recommended that Jordan takes steps to amend legislation or otherwise clarify that a single Constituent Entity of the same MNE Group may be designated to file the CbC report which would satisfy the local filing requirement of all the Constituent Entities in Jordan. Jordan has clarified that a single Constituent Entity may be designated to file the CbC report on behalf of all the Constituent Entities in Jordan and the recommendation is removed.

The surrogate filing provision

Jordan's guidance makes reference to a surrogate parent entity (see above) but does not include any further detail in respect of the circumstances under which surrogate filing is permitted. It is recommended that Jordan clarify the circumstances in which surrogate entity filing is permitted.

Currency Fluctuations

Where an MNE Group draws up, or would draw up, its Consolidated Financial Statements in a currency other than that specified by Jordan, the reference to Jordan's threshold has the effect as if it were a reference to the equivalent in that currency at the average exchange rate for the accounting period. While this provision would not create an issue for MNE Groups whose Ultimate Parent Entity is a tax resident in Jordan, it may be incompatible with the guidance on currency fluctuations for MNE Groups whose Ultimate Parent Entity is located in another jurisdiction, if local filing requirements were applied in respect of a Constituent Entity (which is a Jordan tax resident) of an MNE Group which does not reach the threshold as determined in the jurisdiction of the Ultimate Parent Entity of such a Group.

It is recommended that Jordan clarify that the annual consolidated group revenue threshold calculation rule applies in line with the OECD guidance on currency fluctuations in respect of an MNE Group whose Ultimate Parent Entity is located in a jurisdiction other than Jordan.

The exchange of information framework

Jordan has no bilateral relationships in place for the exchange of CbC reports nor processes to ensure that the exchange of information is conducted in a manner consistent with the terms of reference relating to the exchange of information framework.

It is recommended that Jordan take steps to have qualifying competent authority agreements in effect with jurisdictions of the Inclusive Framework that meet the confidentiality, consistency and appropriate use conditions and with which Jordan has an international exchange of information agreement in effect that allows for the automatic exchange of tax information. This recommendation remains in place since the 2019/2020 peer review.

It is recommended that Jordan take steps to implement the necessary processes or written procedures to ensure that the exchange of information is conducted in a manner consistent with the terms of reference relating to the exchange of information framework. This recommendation remains in place since the 2019/2020 peer review.

Appropriate use of CbC reports

Jordan does not yet have controls in place to ensure the appropriate use of CbC reports.

It is recommended that Jordan take steps to ensure that the appropriate use condition is met ahead of the first exchanges of information. This recommendation remains in place since the 2019/2020 peer review.

Kazakhstan

Overview of CbC reporting requirements

First reporting fiscal year: Commencing on or after 1 January 2016

Consolidated group revenue threshold: EUR 750 million

Filing deadline: 12 months following the end of the reporting fiscal year

Local filing required: Yes

Surrogate parent entity filing permitted: Yes

First review of the domestic legal framework: 2018/2019

Summary of recommendations

Area of implementation	Recommendations for improvement
Domestic legal and administrative framework	It is recommended that Kazakhstan clarify the exact scope, conditions, and legal basis under the minimum standard and/ or the exchange of information framework for the exemption in case of state secrets. It is recommended that Kazakhstan implement a provision whereby a single Constituent Entity of the same MNE Group may be designated to file the CbC report which would satisfy the local filing requirement of all the Constituent Entities in Kazakhstan. It is recommended that Kazakhstan clarify that the annual consolidated group revenue threshold calculation rule applies in line with the OECD guidance on currency fluctuations in respect of an MNE Group whose Ultimate Parent Entity is located in a jurisdiction other than Kazakhstan.
Exchange of information framework	It is recommended that Kazakhstan take steps to implement processes or written procedures to ensure that the exchange of information is conducted in a manner consistent with the terms of reference relating to the exchange of information framework ahead of its first exchanges of information. It is recommended that Kazakhstan take steps to ensure that the number of reports received and exchanged are monitored.
Appropriate use	None.

The domestic legal and administrative framework

It is recommended that Kazakhstan clarify the exact scope, conditions, and legal basis under the minimum standard and/ or the exchange of information framework for the exemption in case of state secrets. This recommendation remains in place since the 2018/2019 peer review.

It is recommended that Kazakhstan implement a provision whereby a single Constituent Entity of the same MNE Group may be designated to file the CbC report which would satisfy the local filing requirement of all the Constituent Entities in Kazakhstan. This recommendation remains in place since the 2018/2019 peer review. [1] [2]

It is recommended that Kazakhstan clarify that the annual consolidated group revenue threshold calculation rule applies in line with the OECD guidance on currency fluctuations in respect of an MNE

Group whose Ultimate Parent Entity is located in a jurisdiction other than Kazakhstan. This recommendation remains in place since the 2022/2023 peer review.

The exchange of information framework

It is recommended that Kazakhstan take steps to implement processes or written procedures to ensure that the exchange of information is conducted in a manner consistent with the terms of reference relating to the exchange of information framework ahead of its first exchanges of information. This recommendation remains in place since the 2018/2019 peer review.

Kazakhstan has not supplied information on the reports it has received from MNE Groups and which it has exchanged on time. It is recommended that Kazakhstan take steps to ensure that the number of reports received and exchanged are monitored.

Appropriate use of CbC reports

Kazakhstan confirms that its rules have not changed and continue to be applied effectively. Kazakhstan continues to meet all terms of reference.

Notes

[1] Kazakhstan's 2018/2019 peer review included a general monitoring point relating to the processes that would allow Kazakhstan to take appropriate measures in case Kazakhstan is notified by another jurisdiction that it has reason to believe with respect to a Reporting Entity that an error may have led to incorrect or incomplete information reporting or that there is non-compliance of a Reporting Entity with respect to its obligation to file a CbC report. This monitoring point remains in place.

[2] Kazakhstan's 2018/2019 peer review included a monitoring point as it is unclear whether Kazakhstan's legislation provides for the deactivation of local filing in case of surrogate filing. Kazakhstan state that this is the case. This monitoring point remains in place.

Kenya

Overview of CbC reporting requirements

First reporting fiscal year: Commencing on or after 1 January 2022

Consolidated group revenue threshold: KES 95 billion

Filing deadline: 12 months following the end of the reporting fiscal year

Local filing required: Yes

Surrogate parent entity filing permitted: Yes

First review of the domestic legal framework: 2022/2023

Summary of recommendations

Area of implementation	Recommendations for improvement
Domestic legal and administrative framework	It is recommended that Kenya amend the filing threshold or otherwise clarify that it is in line with the standard. It is recommended that Kenya amend the definition of Ultimate Parent Entity or otherwise clarify the definition to be in line with the standard. It is recommended that Kenya publish the full content and format requirements of the CbC Report. It is recommended that Kenya clarify that the annual consolidated group revenue threshold calculation rule applies in line with the OECD guidance on currency fluctuations in respect of an MNE Group whose Ultimate Parent Entity is located in a jurisdiction other than Kenya.
Exchange of information framework	It is recommended that Kenya take steps to implement the necessary processes or written procedures to ensure that the exchange of information is conducted in a manner consistent with the terms of reference relating to the exchange of information framework.
Appropriate use	None.

The domestic legal and administrative framework

Kenya's 2022/2023 peer review confirmed that Kenya had introduced legislative amendments but did not include a review of that legislation. These legislative amendments have now been reviewed.[1]

There are a number of areas where there are recommendations to improve the legislation. These recommendations remain in place since the 2022/2023 peer review.

Filing Threshold

Kenya's legislation specifies a filing threshold of KES 95 billion. The minimum standard requires a filing threshold of EUR 750 million or a near equivalent amount in domestic currency as of January 2015. The filing threshold specified in Kenya's legislation is not consistent with this. It is recommended that Kenya amend the filing threshold or otherwise clarify that it is in line with the standard.

Reporting fiscal year

Kenya's 2022/2023 peer review recommended that Kenya takes steps to amend legislation or otherwise clarify that an MNE Group should consider its requirement to file using the consolidated group revenue of its fiscal year immediately preceding a reporting fiscal year for comparison with the threshold. Kenya has amended its legislation to specify that the threshold requirement refers to MNE Groups' consolidated group revenue of its immediately preceding fiscal year and this recommendation is removed.

The definition of Ultimate Parent Entity

The definition in Kenya's legislation refers to an entity that is not controlled by another entity and owns or controls one or more Constituent Entities of an MNE Group. The definition in Kenya's legislation does not adequately capture the requirement to prepare consolidated financial statements, as is required under the standard. Furthermore, the definition in Kenya's legislation also fails to cover circumstances where an entity owns directly or indirectly a sufficient interest in one or more other Constituent Entities such that it would be required to prepare Consolidated Financial Statements if its equity interests were traded on a public securities exchange in its jurisdiction of tax residence (the "deemed listing provision"), which is required under the standard. It is recommended that Kenya amend the definition of UPE or otherwise clarify the definition to be in line with the standard.

Contents of the Country-by-Country report

The information included in the legislation does not include all of the template of the Country-by-Country report and does not include any details of what should be included under each heading in the report. It is recommended that Kenya publish the full content and format requirements of the CbC Report.

The local filing provision

Kenya's 2022/2023 peer review recommended that Kenya takes steps to amend legislation or otherwise clarify that a locally filed CbC report should be filed within 12 months of the end of the reporting period. Kenya has amended its legislation to specify a filing deadline within 12 months after the end of the reporting period for local filing and this recommendation is removed.

Kenya's 2022/2023 peer review recommended that Kenya takes steps to amend legislation or otherwise clarify that local filing only occurs in the circumstances permitted under the minimum standard. Kenya has amended its legislation to ensure that the local filing requirement in Kenya does not apply where a UPE located in a jurisdiction other than Kenya files a report in its jurisdiction of tax residence and that jurisdiction has a qualifying competent authority agreement with Kenya, and the competent authority of that jurisdiction has not notified Kenya of a systemic failure. In addition, Kenya has now met all of the consistency, confidentiality and appropriate use conditions and this recommendation is removed.

Currency Fluctuations

Where an MNE Group draws up, or would draw up, its Consolidated Financial Statements in a currency other than that specified by Kenya, the reference to Kenya's threshold has the effect as if it were a reference to the equivalent in that currency at the average exchange rate for the accounting period. While this provision would not create an issue for MNE Groups whose Ultimate Parent Entity is a tax resident in Kenya, it may be incompatible with the guidance on currency fluctuations for MNE Groups whose Ultimate Parent Entity is located in another jurisdiction, if local filing requirements were applied in respect of a Constituent Entity (which is a Kenya tax resident) of an MNE Group which does not reach the threshold as determined in the jurisdiction of the Ultimate Parent Entity of such a Group.

It is recommended that Kenya clarify that the annual consolidated group revenue threshold calculation rule applies in line with the OECD guidance on currency fluctuations in respect of an MNE Group whose Ultimate Parent Entity is located in a jurisdiction other than Kenya.

The exchange of information framework

Kenya's 2017/2018 peer review included a recommendation that Kenya take steps to have qualifying competent authority agreements in effect with jurisdictions of the Inclusive Framework which meet the confidentiality, consistency and appropriate use conditions and with which Kenya has an international exchange of information agreement in effect that allows for the automatic exchange of tax information. Kenya has now activated relationships under the Multilateral Competent Authority Agreement for exchanging CbC reports and this recommendation is removed.

It is recommended that Kenya take steps to implement the necessary processes or written procedures to ensure that the exchange of information is conducted in a manner consistent with the terms of reference relating to the exchange of information framework. This recommendation remains in place since the 2018/2019 peer review.

Appropriate use of CbC reports

Kenya's 2017/2018 peer review report included a recommendation to take steps to ensure that the appropriate use condition is met ahead of the first exchanges of information. Kenya now has controls in place to ensure the appropriate use of CbC reports and this recommendation is removed.

Kenya meets all terms of reference with respect to the appropriate use condition.

Note

[1] https://kra.go.ke/images/publications/The-Finance-Act--2023.pdf.

Korea

Overview of CbC reporting requirements

First reporting fiscal year: Commencing on or after 1 January 2016

Consolidated group revenue threshold: KRW 1 trillion

Filing deadline: 12 months following the end of the reporting fiscal year

Local filing required: Yes

Surrogate parent entity filing permitted: Yes

First review of the domestic legal framework: 2017/2018

Summary of recommendations

Area of implementation	Recommendations for improvement
Domestic legal and administrative framework	None.
Exchange of information framework	None.
Appropriate use	None.

The domestic legal and administrative framework

Korea confirms that its rules have not changed and continue to be applied effectively. Korea continues to meet all terms of reference.

The exchange of information framework

Korea confirms that its rules have not changed and continue to be applied effectively. Korea continues to meet all terms of reference.

Appropriate use of CbC reports

Korea confirms that its rules have not changed and continue to be applied effectively. Korea continues to meet all terms of reference.

Latvia

Overview of CbC reporting requirements

First reporting fiscal year: Commencing on or after 1 January 2016

Consolidated group revenue threshold: EUR 750 million

Filing deadline: 12 months following the end of the reporting fiscal year

Local filing required: Yes

Surrogate parent entity filing permitted: Yes

First review of the domestic legal framework: 2017/2018

Summary of recommendations

Area of implementation	Recommendations for improvement
Domestic legal and administrative framework	None.
Exchange of information framework	None.
Appropriate use	None.

The domestic legal and administrative framework

Latvia confirms that its rules have not changed and continue to be applied effectively. Latvia continues to meet all terms of reference.

The exchange of information framework

Latvia confirms that its rules have not changed and continue to be applied effectively. Latvia continues to meet all terms of reference.

Appropriate use of CbC reports

Latvia confirms that its rules have not changed and continue to be applied effectively. Latvia continues to meet all terms of reference.

Liberia

Overview of CbC reporting requirements

Liberia has not yet introduced a requirement for the filing of CbC reports, as required under the BEPS Action 13 (CbC reporting) minimum standard.

Summary of recommendations

Area of implementation	Recommendations for improvement
Domestic legal and administrative framework	It is recommended that Liberia take steps to implement a domestic legal and administrative framework to impose and enforce CbC reporting requirements as soon as possible.
Exchange of information framework	It is recommended that Liberia take steps to have qualifying competent authority agreements in effect with jurisdictions of the Inclusive Framework that meet the confidentiality, consistency and appropriate use conditions and with which Liberia has an international exchange of information agreement in effect that allows for the automatic exchange of tax information. It is recommended that Liberia take steps to implement the necessary processes or written procedures to ensure that the exchange of information is conducted in a manner consistent with the terms of reference relating to the exchange of information framework.
Appropriate use	It is recommended that Liberia take steps to ensure that the appropriate use condition is met ahead of the first exchanges of information.

The domestic legal and administrative framework

Liberia does not yet have legislation in place to implement the BEPS Action 13 minimum standard.

It is recommended that Liberia take steps to implement a domestic legal and administrative framework to impose and enforce CbC reporting requirements as soon as possible. This recommendation remains in place since the 2018/2019 peer review.

The exchange of information framework

Liberia has no bilateral relationships in place for the exchange of CbC reports nor processes to ensure that the exchange of information is conducted in a manner consistent with the terms of reference relating to the exchange of information framework.

It is recommended that Liberia take steps to have qualifying competent authority agreements in effect with jurisdictions of the Inclusive Framework that meet the confidentiality, consistency and appropriate use conditions and with which Liberia has an international exchange of information agreement in effect that allows for the automatic exchange of tax information. This recommendation remains in place since the 2018/2019 peer review.

It is recommended that Liberia take steps to implement the necessary processes or written procedures to ensure that the exchange of information is conducted in a manner consistent with the terms of reference relating to the exchange of information framework. This recommendation remains in place since the 2018/2019 peer review.

Appropriate use of CbC reports

Liberia does not yet have controls in place to ensure the appropriate use of CbC reports.

It is recommended that Liberia take steps to ensure that the appropriate use condition is met ahead of the first exchanges of information. This recommendation remains in place since the 2018/2019 peer review.

Liechtenstein

Overview of CbC reporting requirements

First reporting fiscal year: Commencing on or after 1 January 2017. Liechtenstein also allowed MNE Groups to file a CbC report on a voluntary basis, for reporting fiscal years commencing between 1 January 2016 and 31 December 2016.

Consolidated group revenue threshold: CHF 900 million

Filing deadline: 12 months following the end of the reporting fiscal year

Local filing required: Yes

Surrogate parent entity filing permitted: Yes

First review of the domestic legal framework: 2017/2018

Summary of recommendations

Area of implementation	Recommendations for improvement
Domestic legal and administrative framework	None.
Exchange of information framework	None.
Appropriate use	None.

The domestic legal and administrative framework

Liechtenstein confirms that its rules have not changed and continue to be applied effectively. Liechtenstein continues to meet all terms of reference.[1]

The exchange of information framework

Liechtenstein confirms that its rules have not changed and continue to be applied effectively. Liechtenstein continues to meet all terms of reference.

Appropriate use of CbC reports

Liechtenstein confirms that its rules have not changed and continue to be applied effectively. Liechtenstein continues to meet all terms of reference.

Note

[1] Liechtenstein's 2017/2018 peer review included a general monitoring point to ensure that legislation setting out local filing requirements is not interpreted as applying to situations where there is no current international agreement between Liechtenstein and the residence jurisdiction of the Ultimate Parent Entity (which is not permitted under the terms of reference). This monitoring point remains in place.

Lithuania

Overview of CbC reporting requirements

First reporting fiscal year: Commencing on or after 1 January 2016

Consolidated group revenue threshold: EUR 750 million

Filing deadline: 12 months following the end of the reporting fiscal year

Local filing required: Yes

Surrogate parent entity filing permitted: Yes

First review of the domestic legal framework: 2017/2018

Summary of recommendations

Area of implementation	Recommendations for improvement
Domestic legal and administrative framework	None.
Exchange of information framework	None.
Appropriate use	None.

The domestic legal and administrative framework

Lithuania confirms that its rules have not changed and continue to be applied effectively. Lithuania continues to meet all terms of reference.

The exchange of information framework

Lithuania confirms that its rules have not changed and continue to be applied effectively. Lithuania continues to meet all terms of reference.

Appropriate use of CbC reports

Lithuania confirms that its rules have not changed and continue to be applied effectively. Lithuania continues to meet all terms of reference.

Luxembourg

Overview of CbC reporting requirements

First reporting fiscal year: Commencing on or after 1 January 2016

Consolidated group revenue threshold: EUR 750 million

Filing deadline: 12 months following the end of the reporting fiscal year

Local filing required: Yes

Surrogate parent entity filing permitted: Yes

First review of the domestic legal framework: 2017/2018

Summary of recommendations

Area of implementation	Recommendations for improvement
Domestic legal and administrative framework	None.
Exchange of information framework	None.
Appropriate use	None.

The domestic legal and administrative framework

Luxembourg confirms that its rules have not changed and continue to be applied effectively. Luxembourg continues to meet all terms of reference.

The exchange of information framework

Luxembourg confirms that its rules have not changed and continue to be applied effectively. Luxembourg continues to meet all terms of reference.

Appropriate use of CbC reports

Luxembourg confirms that its rules have not changed and continue to be applied effectively. Luxembourg continues to meet all terms of reference.

Macau (China)

Overview of CbC reporting requirements

First reporting fiscal year: Commencing on or after 1 January 2019

Consolidated group revenue threshold: MOP 7 billion

Filing deadline: 12 months following the end of the reporting fiscal year

Local filing required: No

Surrogate parent entity filing permitted: No

First review of the domestic legal framework: 2019/2020

Summary of recommendations

Area of implementation	Recommendations for improvement
Domestic legal and administrative framework	None.
Exchange of information framework	None.
Appropriate use	Not reviewed.

The domestic legal and administrative framework

Macau confirms that its rules have not changed and continue to be applied effectively. Macau continues to meet all terms of reference.

The exchange of information framework

Macau confirms that its rules have not changed and continue to be applied effectively. Macau continues to meet all terms of reference.

Appropriate use of CbC reports

Macau has notified as a non-reciprocal jurisdiction and, as such, will not receive CbC reports submitted to tax authorities in other jurisdictions, and will not apply local filing. It is therefore not necessary for this peer review evaluation to reach any conclusions with respect to Macau's compliance with the terms of reference on appropriate use.

Malaysia

Overview of CbC reporting requirements

First reporting fiscal year: Commencing on or after 1 January 2017. Malaysia also allowed MNE Groups to file a CbC report on a voluntary basis, for reporting fiscal years commencing between 1 January 2016 and 31 December 2016.

Consolidated group revenue threshold: MYR 3 billion

Filing deadline: 12 months following the end of the reporting fiscal year

Local filing required: No

Surrogate parent entity filing permitted: Yes

First review of the domestic legal framework: 2017/2018

Summary of recommendations

Area of implementation	Recommendations for improvement
Domestic legal and administrative framework	None.
Exchange of information framework	None.
Appropriate use	None.

The domestic legal and administrative framework

Malaysia confirms that its rules have not changed and continue to be applied effectively. Malaysia continues to meet all terms of reference.

The exchange of information framework

Malaysia confirms that its rules have not changed and continue to be applied effectively. Malaysia continues to meet all terms of reference.

Appropriate use of CbC reports

Malaysia confirms that its rules have not changed and continue to be applied effectively. Malaysia continues to meet all terms of reference.

Maldives

Overview of CbC reporting requirements

First reporting fiscal year: Commencing on or after 1 January 2021

Consolidated group revenue threshold: EUR 750 million

Filing deadline: 12 months following the end of the reporting fiscal year

Local filing required: Yes

Surrogate parent entity filing permitted: Yes

First review of the domestic legal framework: 2020/2021

Summary of recommendations

Area of implementation	Recommendations for improvement
Domestic legal and administrative framework	None.
Exchange of information framework	None.
Appropriate use	None.

The domestic legal and administrative framework

Maldives previously suspended its local filing requirement. This suspension has now been lifted, and an amendment was published to reinstate local filing.[1]

Maldives confirms that its rules have not changed and continue to be applied effectively. Maldives continues to meet all terms of reference.

The exchange of information framework

Maldives confirms that its rules have not changed and continue to be applied effectively. Maldives continues to meet all terms of reference.

Appropriate use of CbC reports

Maldives confirms that its rules have not changed and continue to be applied effectively. Maldives continues to meet all terms of reference.

Note

[1] https://www.mira.gov.mv/Files/GetFile/699d936a-f6b3-401d-9dc6-e23d09201258

Malta

Overview of CbC reporting requirements

First reporting fiscal year: Commencing on or after 1 January 2016

Consolidated group revenue threshold: EUR 750 million

Filing deadline: 12 months following the end of the reporting fiscal year

Local filing required: Yes, for reporting fiscal years commencing on or after 1 January 2017

Surrogate parent entity filing permitted: Yes

First review of the domestic legal framework: 2017/2018

Summary of recommendations

Area of implementation	Recommendations for improvement
Domestic legal and administrative framework	None.
Exchange of information framework	None.
Appropriate use	None.

The domestic legal and administrative framework

Malta confirms that its rules have not changed and continue to be applied effectively. Malta continues to meet all terms of reference.

The exchange of information framework

Malta confirms that its rules have not changed and continue to be applied effectively. Malta continues to meet all terms of reference.

Appropriate use of CbC reports

Malta confirms that its rules have not changed and continue to be applied effectively. Malta continues to meet all terms of reference.

Mauritania

Overview of CbC reporting requirements

First reporting fiscal year: To be confirmed

Consolidated group revenue threshold: MRO 22 billion

Filing deadline: 12 months following the end of the reporting fiscal year

Local filing required: Yes

Surrogate parent entity filing permitted: Yes

First review of the domestic legal framework: 2022/2023

Summary of recommendations

Area of implementation	Recommendations for improvement
Domestic legal and administrative framework	It is recommended that Mauritania amend the filing threshold or otherwise clarify that it is in line with the standard. It is recommended that Mauritania clarify or amend the legislation to include an effective date for the CbC filing requirement. It is recommended that Mauritania introduce or complete the definitions of a "Group", "MNE Group", "Ultimate Parent Entity", "Constituent Entity", "Consolidated Financial Statements", "Fiscal Year", "Reporting Fiscal Year", "Reporting Entity", and "Systemic Failure" in a manner that is consistent with the terms of reference. It is recommended that Mauritania publish the full content and format requirements of the CbC Report. It is recommended that Mauritania take steps to ensure that local filing only occurs in the circumstances permitted under the minimum standard. It is recommended that Mauritania clarify that the annual consolidated group revenue threshold calculation rule applies in line with the OECD guidance on currency fluctuations in respect of an MNE Group whose Ultimate Parent Entity is located in a jurisdiction other than Mauritania. It is recommended that Mauritania take steps to ensure that enforcement provisions and monitoring relating to the enforcement of CbCR filing obligations are implemented.
Exchange of information framework	It is recommended that Mauritania take steps to have qualifying competent authority agreements in effect with jurisdictions of the Inclusive Framework that meet the confidentiality, consistency and appropriate use conditions and with which Thailand has an international exchange of information agreement in effect that allows for the automatic exchange of tax information. It is recommended that Mauritania take steps to implement the necessary processes or written procedures to ensure that the exchange of information is conducted in a manner consistent with the terms of reference relating to the exchange of information framework.
Appropriate use	It is recommended that Mauritania take steps to ensure that the appropriate use condition is met ahead of the first exchanges of information.

The domestic legal and administrative framework

There are several areas where there are recommendations to improve the legislation. These recommendations remain in place since the 2022/2023 peer review.

Effective date

As Mauritania's legislation does not include an effective date, a legislative filing requirement is therefore not in effect in Mauritania. Mauritania should introduce an effective date in the legislation in order to give effect to the filing requirement.

Filing Threshold

Mauritania's legislation specifies a filing threshold of MRO 22 billion. The minimum standard requires a filing threshold of EUR 750 million or a near equivalent amount in domestic currency as of January 2015. The filing threshold specified in Mauritania's legislation is not consistent with this. It is recommended that Mauritania amend the filing threshold or otherwise clarify that it is in line with the standard.

Effective date

Mauritania's legislation does not include an effective date from which CbC reporting is required. It is recommended that Mauritania clarify or amend the legislation to include an effective date for the CbC filing requirement.

The definition of Group

Mauritania's legislation does not include a definition of "Group". It is recommended that Mauritania amend its legislation to include a definition of "Group" that is in line with the standard.

The definition of MNE Group

Mauritania's legislation does not include a definition of "MNE Group". It is recommended that Mauritania amend its legislation to include a definition of "MNE Group" that is in line with the standard.

The definition of Ultimate Parent Entity

The definition of "Ultimate Parent Entity" in Mauritania's legislation refers to a legal person being required to prepare consolidated financial statements under accounting principles, but it does not include an entity that would be required to prepare consolidated financial statements if its equity interests were traded on a public securities exchange in Mauritania ("deemed listing provision"), as required under the standard. In addition, it is unclear whether the first condition relates to an obligation to prepare consolidated financial statements under accounting principles applicable in Mauritania or whether it could apply to legal persons that prepare such statements without being required to do so. It is also unclear whether the legislation would apply to entities which do not have legal personality.

Under the terms of reference, the Ultimate Parent Entity shall not be held by another Constituent Entity that owns directly or indirectly sufficient interest to be considered as an Ultimate Parent Entity. This is not reflected in Mauritania's primary law, which instead contains the following conditions in the primary filing obligation provisions: the Ultimate Parent Entity is "*not held by one or more legal entities located in Mauritania which are subject to the filing of this declaration, or established outside Mauritania and required to file a similar declaration under foreign regulations*". It appears that these provisions may in fact trigger a primary filing obligation on a Constituent Entity in Mauritania which would not be considered the Ultimate Parent Entity under the terms of reference, where the actual Ultimate Parent Entity under the terms of reference is not required to file a CbC report. In effect, this is an instance of local filing for entities in Mauritania when there is no requirement to file CbC report on an entity located in another jurisdiction, which would be considered as their Ultimate Parent Entity as per the standard (this may technically give rise to a duplication of the CbC reports filed under both the primary and secondary filing requirements by the parent company in Mauritania). Where such a local filing obligation occurs, there are no provisions (i) which would allow an MNE Group to designate one Constituent Entity to file the CbC report and (ii) which would deactivate this filing obligation when a CbC report is made available through surrogate filing.

In light of the above, it is recommended that Mauritania amend the definition of UPE or otherwise clarify the definition to be in line with the standard.

The definition of Constituent Entity

Mauritania's legislation does not include a definition of "Constituent Entity". It is recommended that Mauritania amend its legislation to include a definition of "Constituent Entity" that is in line with the standard.

The definition of Consolidated Financial Statements

Mauritania's legislation does not include a definition of "Consolidated Financial Statements". It is recommended that Mauritania amend its legislation to include a definition of "Consolidated Financial Statements" that is in line with the standard.

The definition of Fiscal Year

Mauritania's legislation does not include a definition of "Fiscal Year". It is recommended that Mauritania amend its legislation to include a definition of "Fiscal Year" that is in line with the standard.

The definition of Reporting Fiscal Year

Mauritania's legislation does not include a definition of "Reporting Fiscal Year". It is recommended that Mauritania amend its legislation to include a definition of "Reporting Fiscal Year" that is in line with the standard.

The definition of Reporting Entity

Mauritania's legislation does not include a definition of "Reporting Entity". It is recommended that Mauritania amend its legislation to include a definition of "Reporting Entity" that is in line with the standard.

The definition of Systemic Failure

Mauritania's legislation does not include a definition of "Systemic Failure". It is recommended that Mauritania amend its legislation to include a definition of "Systemic Failure" that is in line with the standard.

Contents of the Country-by-Country report

The information included in Mauritania's legislation does not include the template of the Country-by-Country report and does not include any details of what should be included under each heading in the report. It is recommended that Mauritania publish the full content and format requirements of the CbC Report.

The local filing provision

The local filing provision in Mauritania applies where an MNE Group has a Constituent Entity established in Mauritania which is not the Ultimate Parent Entity of the group, and the jurisdiction of residence of the Ultimate Parent Entity of the MNE Group does not have an international agreement with Mauritania allowing the automatic exchange of CbC reports. This is broader than the condition under the standard, where a jurisdiction may require local filing if "the jurisdiction in which the Ultimate Parent Entity is resident for tax purposes has a current International Agreement to which the given jurisdiction is a party but does not have a Qualifying Competent Authority Agreement in effect to which this jurisdiction is a party by the time for filing the Country-by-Country Report". Under Mauritania's legislation, local filing may be required in circumstances where there is no current international agreement between Mauritania and the residence jurisdiction of the Ultimate Parent Entity. It is recommended that Mauritania amend its primary law or otherwise ensure that local filing only occurs in the circumstances permitted under the minimum standard, in particular to prevent local filing in the absence on an international agreement.

With respect to the conditions under which local filing may be required, under Mauritania's legislation, local filing applies where an MNE group has a Constituent Entity established in Mauritania which is not the Ultimate Parent Entity of the Group, and the jurisdiction of the Ultimate Parent Entity has concluded an agreement with Mauritania for the automatic exchange of CbC reports but does not comply with the obligations arising from such agreement. Whether these provisions fully reflect the standard which limit local filing to the instances of "Systemic Failure" (i.e. suspension for reasons other than those that are in accordance with the terms of that agreement or persistent failure to automatically provide the CbC report) should be clarified. It is recommended that Mauritania amend its primary legislation or otherwise clarify that local filing will only apply if there is a "Systemic Failure".

Mauritania has a legislative requirement for local filing which is in effect despite Mauritania not yet meeting all of the consistency, confidentiality and appropriate use conditions. It is therefore recommended that Mauritania take steps to ensure that local filing only occurs in the circumstances permitted under the minimum standard.

Limitation on local filing in case of surrogate filing

Mauritania's local filing requirements will not apply if there is surrogate filing in another jurisdiction which is listed in a list of states or territories which have adopted regulations imposing the filing of a CbC report similar to that required in Mauritania, which have concluded an agreement with Mauritania for the automatic exchange of CbC reports and which comply with the obligations arising from such agreement. It is unclear whether local filing would be "deactivated" in respect of jurisdictions which allow voluntary parent surrogate filing, being noted that the list mentioned above has not yet been published at this point in time. This will be monitored.

Currency fluctuations

It is recommended that Mauritania clarify that the annual consolidated group revenue threshold calculation rule applies in line with the OECD guidance on currency fluctuations in respect of an MNE Group whose Ultimate Parent Entity is located in a jurisdiction other than Mauritania.

Effective implementation

Mauritania does not have a legal mechanism in place to enforce compliance with the minimum standard. It is recommended that Mauritania take steps to ensure that enforcement provisions and monitoring relating to the enforcement of CbCR filing obligations are implemented.

Mauritania does not have a process to take appropriate measures in case it is notified by another jurisdiction that such other jurisdiction has reason to believe that an error may have led to incorrect or incomplete information reporting by a Reporting Entity or that there is non-compliance of a Reporting Entity with respect to its obligation to file a CbC report. As no exchange of CbC reports has yet occurred no recommendation is made but this aspect will be further monitored.

The exchange of information framework

Mauritania has no bilateral relationships in place for the exchange of CbC reports nor processes to ensure that the exchange of information is conducted in a manner consistent with the terms of reference relating to the exchange of information framework.

It is recommended that Mauritania take steps to have qualifying competent authority agreements in effect with jurisdictions of the Inclusive Framework that meet the confidentiality, consistency and appropriate use conditions and with which Mauritania has an international exchange of information agreement in effect that allows for the automatic exchange of tax information.

It is recommended that Mauritania take steps to implement the necessary processes or written procedures to ensure that the exchange of information is conducted in a manner consistent with the terms of reference relating to the exchange of information framework.

These recommendations remain in place since the 2022/2023 peer review.

Appropriate use of CbC reports

Mauritania does not yet have controls in place to ensure the appropriate use of CbC reports.

It is recommended that Mauritania take steps to ensure that the appropriate use condition is met ahead of the first exchanges of information.

This recommendation remains in place since the 2022/2023 peer review.

Mauritius

Overview of CbC reporting requirements

First reporting fiscal year: Commencing on or after 1 July 2018.

Consolidated group revenue threshold: EUR 750 million

Filing deadline: 12 months following the end of the reporting fiscal year

Local filing required: No

Surrogate parent entity filing permitted: Yes

First review of the domestic legal framework: 2018/2019

Summary of recommendations

Area of implementation	Recommendations for improvement
Domestic legal and administrative framework	None.
Exchange of information framework	None.
Appropriate use	None.

The domestic legal and administrative framework

Mauritius confirms that its rules have not changed and continue to be applied effectively. Mauritius continues to meet all terms of reference.

The exchange of information framework

Mauritius confirms that its rules have not changed and continue to be applied effectively. Mauritius continues to meet all terms of reference.

Appropriate use of CbC reports

Mauritius confirms that its rules have not changed and continue to be applied effectively. Mauritius continues to meet all terms of reference.

Mexico

Overview of CbC reporting requirements

First reporting fiscal year: Commencing on or after 1 January 2016

Consolidated group revenue threshold: MXN 12 billion

Filing deadline: 12 months following the end of the reporting fiscal year

Local filing required: Yes

Surrogate parent entity filing permitted: Yes

First review of the domestic legal framework: 2017/2018

Summary of recommendations

Area of implementation	Recommendations for improvement
Domestic legal and administrative framework	None.
Exchange of information framework	None.
Appropriate use	None.

The domestic legal and administrative framework

Mexico confirms that its rules have not changed and continue to be applied effectively. Mexico continues to meet all terms of reference.[1] [2]

The exchange of information framework

Mexico confirms that its rules have not changed and continue to be applied effectively. Mexico continues to meet all terms of reference.

Appropriate use of CbC reports

Mexico confirms that its rules have not changed and continue to be applied effectively. Mexico continues to meet all terms of reference.

Notes

[1] Mexico's 2017/2018 peer review included a general monitoring point with respect to the annual consolidated group revenue threshold under article 76-A, paragraph III.c.6. of the Mexican Income Tax

Law, which may be inconsistent with paragraph 8 a) ii. of the terms of reference, as it may generate fluctuations from year to year on the threshold to require the filing of CbC reports. Mexico indicates that the sole purpose of this provision is to have a legal vehicle in order change the threshold if such change arises from the 2020 revision. Mexico confirms that there were no yearly fluctuations to the annual consolidated group revenue threshold under article 76-A during the year in review. This monitoring point remains in place.

[2] Mexico's 2017/2018 peer review included a monitoring point relating to the definition of "number of employees" in its legislation. The definition in Mexico's legislation does not mirror the Action 13 Report's specific instructions by not providing flexibility to taxpayers to report independent contractors as employees. However, this does not seem to raise any significant concern, taking into account the particular domestic context as described by Mexico. Mexico confirms that the definition of "number of employees" remains as established since it is intended to address specific issues related to certain tax planning setups relevant in the Mexican context. This monitoring point remains in place.

Monaco

Overview of CbC reporting requirements

First reporting fiscal year: Commencing on or after 1 January 2018

Consolidated group revenue threshold: EUR 750 million

Filing deadline: 12 months following the end of the reporting fiscal year

Local filing required: No

Surrogate parent entity filing permitted: Yes

First review of the domestic legal framework: 2017/2018

Summary of recommendations

Area of implementation	Recommendations for improvement
Domestic legal and administrative framework	None.
Exchange of information framework	None.
Appropriate use	None.

The domestic legal and administrative framework

Monaco confirms that its rules have not changed and continue to be applied effectively. Monaco continues to meet all terms of reference.

The exchange of information framework

Monaco confirms that its rules have not changed and continue to be applied effectively. Monaco continues to meet all terms of reference.

Appropriate use of CbC reports

Monaco confirms that its rules have not changed and continue to be applied effectively. Monaco continues to meet all terms of reference.

Mongolia

Overview of CbC reporting requirements

First reporting fiscal year: Commencing on or after 1 January 2020

Consolidated group revenue threshold: MNT 1.7 trillion

Filing deadline: 12 months following the end of the reporting fiscal year

Local filing required: Yes

Surrogate parent entity filing permitted: Yes

First review of the domestic legal framework: 2020/2021

Summary of recommendations

Area of implementation	Recommendations for improvement
Domestic legal and administrative framework	It is recommended that Mongolia take steps to ensure that local filing only occurs in the circumstances permitted under the minimum standard. It is recommended that Mongolia clarify that the annual consolidated group revenue threshold calculation rule applies in line with the OECD guidance on currency fluctuations in respect of an MNE Group whose Ultimate Parent Entity is located in a jurisdiction other than Mongolia.
Exchange of information framework	It is recommended that Mongolia take steps to have qualifying competent authority agreements in effect with jurisdictions of the Inclusive Framework that meet the confidentiality, consistency and appropriate use conditions and with which Mongolia has an international exchange of information agreement in effect that allows for the automatic exchange of tax information. It is recommended that Mongolia take steps to implement the necessary processes or written procedures to ensure that the exchange of information is conducted in a manner consistent with the terms of reference relating to the exchange of information framework.
Appropriate use	It is recommended that Mongolia take steps to ensure that the appropriate use condition is met ahead of the first exchanges of information.

The domestic legal and administrative framework

It is recommended that Mongolia take steps to ensure that local filing only occurs in the circumstances permitted under the minimum standard. This recommendation remains in place since the 2020/2021 peer review.

It is recommended that Mongolia clarify that the annual consolidated group revenue threshold calculation rule applies in line with the OECD guidance on currency fluctuations in respect of an MNE Group whose Ultimate Parent Entity is located in a jurisdiction other than Mongolia. This recommendation remains in place since the 2020/2021 peer review.

Mongolia's domestic legal and administrative framework meets all other terms of reference.

The exchange of information framework

Mongolia has no bilateral relationships in place for the exchange of CbC reports nor processes to ensure that the exchange of information is conducted in a manner consistent with the terms of reference relating to the exchange of information framework.

It is recommended that Mongolia take steps to have qualifying competent authority agreements in effect with jurisdictions of the Inclusive Framework that meet the confidentiality, consistency and appropriate use conditions and with which Mongolia has an international exchange of information agreement in effect that allows for the automatic exchange of tax information. This recommendation remains in place since the 2018/2019 peer review.

It is recommended that Mongolia take steps to implement the necessary processes or written procedures to ensure that the exchange of information is conducted in a manner consistent with the terms of reference relating to the exchange of information framework. This recommendation remains in place since the 2018/2019 peer review.

Appropriate use of CbC reports

Mongolia does not yet have controls in place to ensure the appropriate use of CbC reports.

It is recommended that Mongolia take steps to ensure that the appropriate use condition is met ahead of the first exchanges of information. This recommendation remains in place since the 2018/2019 peer review.

Montenegro

Overview of CbC reporting requirements

First reporting fiscal year: Commencing on or after 1 January 2024

Consolidated group revenue threshold: EUR 750 million

Filing deadline: 12 months following the end of the reporting fiscal year

Local filing required: Yes

Surrogate parent entity filing permitted: Yes

First review of the domestic legal framework: 2022/2023

Summary of recommendations

Area of implementation	Recommendations for improvement
Domestic legal and administrative framework	It is recommended that Montenegro introduce or complete the definitions of a "Reporting Entity", "Qualifying Competent Authority Agreement", "International Agreement", and "Systemic Failure" in a manner that is consistent with the terms of reference.
	It is recommended that Montenegro take steps to ensure that local filing only occurs in the circumstances permitted under the minimum standard.
	It is recommended that Montenegro implement a provision whereby a single Constituent Entity of the same MNE Group may be designated to file the CbC report which would satisfy the local filing requirement of all the Constituent Entities in Montenegro.
	It is recommended that Montenegro clarify that the annual consolidated group revenue threshold calculation rule applies in line with the OECD guidance on currency fluctuations in respect of an MNE Group whose Ultimate Parent Entity is located in a jurisdiction other than Montenegro.
Exchange of information framework	It is recommended that Montenegro take steps to implement the necessary processes or written procedures to ensure that the exchange of information is conducted in a manner consistent with the terms of reference relating to the exchange of information framework.
Appropriate use	It is recommended that Montenegro take steps to ensure that the appropriate use condition is met ahead of the first exchanges of information.

The domestic legal and administrative framework

Montenegro has a number of recommendations to improve the legislation. These recommendations remain in place since the 2022/2023 peer review.[1]

The definition of Reporting Entity

Montenegro's legislation does not include a definition of "Reporting Entity". It is recommended that Montenegro amend its legislation to include a definition of "Reporting Entity" that is in line with the standard.

The definition of Qualifying Competent Authority Agreement

Montenegro's legislation does not include a definition of "Qualifying Competent Authority Agreement". It is recommended that Montenegro amend its legislation to include a definition of "Qualifying Competent Authority Agreement" that is in line with the standard.

The definition of International Agreement

The definition in Montenegro's legislation refers to an agreement that Montenegro has concluded in written form with one or several states or with one or several international organisations, under the regulations of international law.

The definition of international agreement is intended to include reference to an agreement which provides legal authority for the exchange of tax information between jurisdictions, including automatic exchange of such information". It is recommended that Montenegro amend the definition of "International Agreement" or otherwise clarify that is in line with the standard.

The definition of Systemic Failure

The definition in Montenegro's legislation refers to meaning that either that a tax jurisdiction has a Qualifying Competent Authority Agreement in effect with Montenegro but has suspended automatic exchange, or that a jurisdiction is otherwise not required to automatically provide to Montenegro reports in its possession of MNE Groups that have Constituent Entities in Montenegro.

The definition of "Systemic Failure" is not intended to extend to where a jurisdiction is otherwise not required to automatically provide to Montenegro reports in its possession of MNE Groups that have Constituent Entities in Montenegro. It is recommended that Montenegro amend the definition of "Systemic Failure" or otherwise clarify that is in line with the standard.

The local filing provision

Montenegro has a legislative requirement which is in effect despite Montenegro not yet meeting all of the consistency, confidentiality and appropriate use conditions. It is therefore recommended that Montenegro take steps to ensure that local filing only occurs in the circumstances permitted under the minimum standard.

Single entity filing

It is recommended that Montenegro implement a provision whereby a single Constituent Entity of the same MNE Group may be designated to file the CbC report which would satisfy the local filing requirement of all the Constituent Entities in Montenegro.

Currency Fluctuations

Where an MNE Group draws up, or would draw up, its Consolidated Financial Statements in a currency other than that specified by Montenegro, the reference to Montenegro's threshold has the effect as if it were a reference to the equivalent in that currency at the average exchange rate for the accounting period. While this provision would not create an issue for MNE Groups whose Ultimate Parent Entity is a tax resident in Montenegro, it may be incompatible with the guidance on currency fluctuations for MNE Groups whose Ultimate Parent Entity is located in another jurisdiction, if local filing requirements were applied in respect of a Constituent Entity (which is a Montenegro tax resident) of an MNE Group which does not reach the threshold as determined in the jurisdiction of the Ultimate Parent Entity of such a Group.

It is recommended that Montenegro clarify that the annual consolidated group revenue threshold calculation rule applies in line with the OECD guidance on currency fluctuations in respect of an MNE Group whose Ultimate Parent Entity is located in a jurisdiction other than Montenegro.

The exchange of information framework

Montenegro's 2021/2022 peer review included a recommendation that Montenegro take steps to have qualifying competent authority agreements in effect with jurisdictions of the Inclusive Framework which meet the confidentiality, consistency and appropriate use conditions and with which Montenegro has an international exchange of information agreement in effect that allows for the automatic exchange of tax information. Montenegro has now activated relationships under the Multilateral Competent Authority Agreement for exchanging CbC reports and this recommendation is removed.

It is recommended that Montenegro take steps to implement the necessary processes or written procedures to ensure that the exchange of information is conducted in a manner consistent with the terms of reference relating to the exchange of information framework. This recommendation remains in place since the 2021/2022 peer review.

Appropriate use of CbC reports

Montenegro does not yet have controls in place to ensure the appropriate use of CbC reports.

It is recommended that Montenegro take steps to ensure that the appropriate use condition is met ahead of the first exchanges of information. This recommendation remains in place since the 2021/2022 peer review.

Note

[1] Montenegro's 2022/2023 peer review included a monitoring point relating to its primary legislation imposing a filing obligation on a "legal person". This definition could be interpreted more narrowly than the standard. Montenegro has indicated that its definition of Ultimate Parent Entity is consistent with the minimum standard. This monitoring point remains in place.

Montserrat

Overview of CbC reporting requirements

First reporting fiscal year: Commencing on or after 1 January 2024

Consolidated group revenue threshold: EUR 750 million

Filing deadline: 12 months following the end of the reporting fiscal year

Local filing required: No

Surrogate parent entity filing permitted: No

First review of the domestic legal framework: 2022/2023

Summary of recommendations

Area of implementation	Recommendations for improvement
Domestic legal and administrative framework	None.
Exchange of information framework	None.
Appropriate use	Not reviewed.

The domestic legal and administrative framework

Montserrat confirms that its rules have not changed and continue to be applied effectively. Montserrat continues to meet all terms of reference.

The exchange of information framework

Montserrat confirms that its rules have not changed and continue to be applied effectively. Montserrat continues to meet all terms of reference.

Appropriate use of CbC reports

Montserrat has notified as a non-reciprocal jurisdiction and, as such, will not receive CbC reports submitted to tax authorities in other jurisdictions. It is therefore not necessary for this peer review evaluation to reach any conclusions with respect to Montserrat's compliance with the terms of reference on appropriate use.

Morocco

Overview of CbC reporting requirements

First reporting fiscal year: Commencing on or after 1 January 2021

Consolidated group revenue threshold: MAD 8 122 500 thousand

Filing deadline: 12 months following the end of the reporting fiscal year

Local filing required: Requirement suspended

Surrogate parent entity filing permitted: Yes

First review of the domestic legal framework: 2020/2021

Summary of recommendations

Area of implementation	Recommendations for improvement
Domestic legal and administrative framework	None.
Exchange of information framework	It is recommended that Morocco take steps to have qualifying competent authority agreements in effect with jurisdictions of the Inclusive Framework that meet the confidentiality, consistency and appropriate use conditions and with which Morocco has an international exchange of information agreement in effect that allows for the automatic exchange of tax information.
Appropriate use	None.

The domestic legal and administrative framework

Morocco confirms that its rules have not changed and continue to be applied effectively. Morocco continues to meet all terms of reference.

The exchange of information framework

Morocco has no bilateral relationships in place for the exchange of CbC reports nor processes to ensure that the exchange of information is conducted in a manner consistent with the terms of reference relating to the exchange of information framework.

It is recommended that Morocco take steps to have qualifying competent authority agreements in effect with jurisdictions of the Inclusive Framework that meet the confidentiality, consistency and appropriate use conditions and with which Morocco has an international exchange of information agreement in effect that allows for the automatic exchange of tax information. This recommendation remains in place since the 2019/2020 peer review.

Morocco's 2019/2020 peer review recommended that Morocco take steps to implement the necessary processes or written procedures to ensure that the exchange of information is conducted in a manner consistent with the terms of reference relating to the exchange of information framework. These processes are now in place and the recommendation is removed.

Appropriate use of CbC reports

Morocco's 2019/2020 peer review report included a recommendation to take steps to ensure that the appropriate use condition is met ahead of the first exchanges of information. Morocco now has controls in place to ensure the appropriate use of CbC reports and this recommendation is removed.

Morocco meets all terms of reference with respect to the appropriate use condition.

Namibia

Overview of CbC reporting requirements

Namibia has not yet introduced a requirement for the filing of CbC reports, as required under the BEPS Action 13 (CbC reporting) minimum standard.

Summary of recommendations

Area of implementation	Recommendations for improvement
Domestic legal and administrative framework	It is recommended that Namibia take steps to implement a domestic legal and administrative framework to impose and enforce CbC reporting requirements as soon as possible.
Exchange of information framework	It is recommended that Namibia take steps to have qualifying competent authority agreements in effect with jurisdictions of the Inclusive Framework that meet the confidentiality, consistency and appropriate use conditions and with which Namibia has an international exchange of information agreement in effect that allows for the automatic exchange of tax information. It is recommended that Namibia take steps to implement the necessary processes or written procedures to ensure that the exchange of information is conducted in a manner consistent with the terms of reference relating to the exchange of information framework.
Appropriate use	It is recommended that Namibia take steps to ensure that the appropriate use condition is met ahead of the first exchanges of information.

The domestic legal and administrative framework

Namibia does not yet have legislation in place to implement the BEPS Action 13 minimum standard.

It is recommended that Namibia take steps to implement a domestic legal and administrative framework to impose and enforce CbC reporting requirements as soon as possible. This recommendation remains in place since the 2019/2020 peer review.

The exchange of information framework

Namibia has no bilateral relationships in place for the exchange of CbC reports nor processes to ensure that the exchange of information is conducted in a manner consistent with the terms of reference relating to the exchange of information framework.

It is recommended that Namibia take steps to have qualifying competent authority agreements in effect with jurisdictions of the Inclusive Framework that meet the confidentiality, consistency and appropriate use conditions and with which Namibia has an international exchange of information agreement in effect that allows for the automatic exchange of tax information. This recommendation remains in place since the 2019/2020 peer review.

It is recommended that Namibia take steps to implement the necessary processes or written procedures to ensure that the exchange of information is conducted in a manner consistent with the terms of reference relating to the exchange of information framework. This recommendation remains in place since the 2019/2020 peer review.

Appropriate use of CbC reports

Namibia does not yet have controls in place to ensure the appropriate use of CbC reports.

It is recommended that Namibia take steps to ensure that the appropriate use condition is met ahead of the first exchanges of information. This recommendation remains in place since the 2019/2020 peer review.

Netherlands

Overview of CbC reporting requirements

First reporting fiscal year: Commencing on or after 1 January 2016

Consolidated group revenue threshold: EUR 750 million

Filing deadline: 12 months following the end of the reporting fiscal year

Local filing required: Yes

Surrogate parent entity filing permitted: Yes

First review of the domestic legal framework: 2017/2018

Summary of recommendations

Area of implementation	Recommendations for improvement
Domestic legal and administrative framework	None.
Exchange of information framework	None.
Appropriate use	None.

The domestic legal and administrative framework

The Netherlands confirms that its rules have not changed and continue to be applied effectively. The Netherlands continues to meet all terms of reference.

The exchange of information framework

The Netherlands made an exchange of CbC reports after the deadline due to a technical issue with its exchange of information portal. This issue has been resolved, and so no recommendation is required.

The Netherlands confirms that its rules have not changed and continue to be applied effectively. The Netherlands continues to meet all terms of reference.

Appropriate use of CbC reports

The Netherlands confirms that its rules have not changed and continue to be applied effectively. The Netherlands continues to meet all terms of reference.

New Zealand

Overview of CbC reporting requirements

First reporting fiscal year: Commencing on or after 1 January 2016

Consolidated group revenue threshold: EUR 750 million

Filing deadline: 12 months following the end of the reporting fiscal year

Local filing required: No

Surrogate parent entity filing permitted: Yes

First review of the domestic legal framework: 2017/2018

Summary of recommendations

Area of implementation	Recommendations for improvement
Domestic legal and administrative framework	None.
Exchange of information framework	None.
Appropriate use	None.

The domestic legal and administrative framework

New Zealand confirms that its rules have not changed and continue to be applied effectively. New Zealand continues to meet all terms of reference.[1]

The exchange of information framework

New Zealand confirms that its rules have not changed and continue to be applied effectively. New Zealand continues to meet all terms of reference.

Appropriate use of CbC reports

New Zealand confirms that its rules have not changed and continue to be applied effectively. New Zealand continues to meet all terms of reference.

Note

[1] The definition of a "large multinational group" in the legislation does not include the "deemed listing provision" as required under the terms of reference. However, New Zealand notes that the financial

reporting requirements in New Zealand apply to large entities (including companies, partnerships and limited partnerships) regardless of whether they are listed on a stock exchange. A "large entity" is defined in the Financial Reporting Act 2013 as an entity that earns over NZD 30 million of consolidated revenues (which is much lower than EUR 750 million) or that have over NZD 60 milion of consolidated assets in the previous two years. New Zealand also confirms that in the very unlikely event that an entity did not prepare consolidated financial statements and would be considered as an "Ultimate Parent Entity" further to the "deemed listing provision" (as per paragraph 18.i. of the terms of reference), the existing powers of Section 17B of the Tax Administration Act 1994 will be relied on to request the information. This monitoring point remains in place.

Nigeria

Overview of CbC reporting requirements

First reporting fiscal year: Commencing on or after 1 January 2018

Consolidated group revenue threshold: NGN 160 billion

Filing deadline: 12 months following the end of the reporting fiscal year

Local filing required: Yes

Surrogate parent entity filing permitted: Yes

First review of the domestic legal framework: 2017/2018

Summary of recommendations

Area of implementation	Recommendations for improvement
Domestic legal and administrative framework	None.
Exchange of information framework	None.
Appropriate use	None.

The domestic legal and administrative framework

Nigeria has reintroduced its local filing requirement.[1]

Nigeria confirms that its rules have not changed and continue to be applied effectively. Nigeria continues to meet all terms of reference.

The exchange of information framework

The 2018/2019 peer review recommended that Nigeria take steps to implement the necessary processes or written procedures to ensure that the exchange of information is conducted in a manner consistent with the terms of reference relating to the exchange of information framework. These processes are now in place and the recommendation is removed.

Appropriate use of CbC reports

Nigeria confirms that its rules have not changed and continue to be applied effectively. Nigeria continues to meet all terms of reference.

[1] https://firs.gov.ng/pdf/FIRS_Local_Filing_2022.pdf

North Macedonia (Republic of)

Overview of CbC reporting requirements

The Republic of North Macedonia (North Macedonia) has not yet introduced a requirement for the filing of CbC reports, as required under the BEPS Action 13 (CbC reporting) minimum standard.

Summary of recommendations

Area of implementation	Recommendations for improvement
Domestic legal and administrative framework	It is recommended that North Macedonia take steps to implement a domestic legal and administrative framework to impose and enforce CbC reporting requirements as soon as possible.
Exchange of information framework	It is recommended that North Macedonia take steps to have qualifying competent authority agreements in effect with jurisdictions of the Inclusive Framework that meet the confidentiality, consistency and appropriate use conditions and with which North Macedonia has an international exchange of information agreement in effect that allows for the automatic exchange of tax information. It is recommended that North Macedonia take steps to implement the necessary processes or written procedures to ensure that the exchange of information is conducted in a manner consistent with the terms of reference relating to the exchange of information framework.
Appropriate use	It is recommended that North Macedonia take steps to ensure that the appropriate use condition is met ahead of the first exchanges of information.

The domestic legal and administrative framework

North Macedonia does not yet have legislation in place to implement the BEPS Action 13 minimum standard.

It is recommended that North Macedonia take steps to implement a domestic legal and administrative framework to impose and enforce CbC reporting requirements as soon as possible. This recommendation remains in place since the 2018/2019 peer review.

The exchange of information framework

North Macedonia has no bilateral relationships in place for the exchange of CbC reports nor processes to ensure that the exchange of information is conducted in a manner consistent with the terms of reference relating to the exchange of information framework.

It is recommended that North Macedonia take steps to have qualifying competent authority agreements in effect with jurisdictions of the Inclusive Framework that meet the confidentiality, consistency and appropriate use conditions and with which North Macedonia has an international exchange of information agreement in effect that allows for the automatic exchange of tax information. This recommendation remains in place since the 2018/2019 peer review.

It is recommended that North Macedonia take steps to implement the necessary processes or written procedures to ensure that the exchange of information is conducted in a manner consistent with the terms

of reference relating to the exchange of information framework. This recommendation remains in place since the 2018/2019 peer review.

Appropriate use of CbC reports

North Macedonia does not yet have controls in place to ensure the appropriate use of CbC reports.

It is recommended that North Macedonia take steps to ensure that the appropriate use condition is met ahead of the first exchanges of information. This recommendation remains in place since the 2018/2019 peer review.

Norway

Overview of CbC reporting requirements

First reporting fiscal year: Commencing on or after 1 January 2016

Consolidated group revenue threshold: NOK 6.5 billion

Filing deadline: 12 months following the end of the reporting fiscal year

Local filing required: Yes

Surrogate parent entity filing permitted: Yes

First review of the domestic legal framework: 2017/2018

Summary of recommendations

Area of implementation	Recommendations for improvement
Domestic legal and administrative framework	None.
Exchange of information framework	None.
Appropriate use	None.

The domestic legal and administrative framework

Norway confirms that its rules have not changed and continue to be applied effectively. Norway continues to meet all terms of reference.[1]

The exchange of information framework

Norway confirms that its rules have not changed and continue to be applied effectively. Norway continues to meet all terms of reference.

Appropriate use of CbC reports

Norway confirms that its rules have not changed and continue to be applied effectively. Norway continues to meet all terms of reference.

Note

[1] Norway's 2017/2018 peer review included a monitoring point relating to the interpretation of the concept of "Systemic Failure". This monitoring point remains in place.

Oman

Overview of CbC reporting requirements

First reporting fiscal year: Commencing on or after 1 January 2020

Consolidated group revenue threshold: OMR 300 million

Filing deadline: 12 months following the end of the reporting fiscal year

Local filing required: Requirement suspended

Surrogate parent entity filing permitted: Yes

First review of the domestic legal framework: 2020/2021

Summary of recommendations

Area of implementation	Recommendations for improvement
Domestic legal and administrative framework	None.
Exchange of information framework	None.
Appropriate use	Not reviewed.

The domestic legal and administrative framework

Oman confirms that its rules have not changed and continue to be applied effectively. Oman continues to meet all terms of reference.

The exchange of information framework

Oman confirms that its rules have not changed and continue to be applied effectively. Oman continues to meet all terms of reference.

Appropriate use of CbC reports

Oman is a non-reciprocal jurisdiction and, as such, will not receive CbC reports submitted to tax authorities in other jurisdictions, and will not apply local filing. It is not necessary for this peer review evaluation to reach any conclusion with respect to Oman's compliance with the terms of reference on appropriate use.

Pakistan

Overview of CbC reporting requirements

First reporting fiscal year: Commencing on or after 1 January 2016

Consolidated group revenue threshold: EUR 750 million

Filing deadline: 12 months following the end of the reporting fiscal year

Local filing required: Yes, for reporting fiscal years commencing on or after 1 January 2017

Surrogate parent entity filing permitted: Yes

First review of the domestic legal framework: 2017/2018

Summary of recommendations

Area of implementation	Recommendations for improvement
Domestic legal and administrative framework	It is recommended that Pakistan clarify that the annual consolidated group revenue threshold calculation rule applies in line with the OECD guidance on currency fluctuations in respect of an MNE Group whose Ultimate Parent Entity is located in a jurisdiction other than Pakistan.
Exchange of information framework	It is recommended that Pakistan take steps to implement processes or written procedures to ensure that the exchange of information is conducted in a manner consistent with the terms of reference relating to the exchange of information framework. It is recommended that Pakistan introduce changes to ensure missing or incomplete information will be identifiable in advance of exchange.
Appropriate use	None.

The domestic legal and administrative framework

It is recommended that Pakistan clarify that the annual consolidated group revenue threshold calculation rule applies in line with the OECD guidance on currency fluctuations in respect of an MNE Group whose Ultimate Parent Entity is located in a jurisdiction other than Pakistan. This recommendation remains in place since the 2022/2023 peer review.

The exchange of information framework

It is recommended that Pakistan take steps to implement processes or written procedures to ensure that the exchange of information is conducted in a manner consistent with the terms of reference relating to the exchange of information framework. This recommendation remains in place since the 2018/2019 peer review.

Peer input was received for Pakistan about missing or incomplete information in CbC reports sent to another jurisdiction. It is recommended that Pakistan introduce changes to ensure missing or incomplete information will be identifiable in advance of exchange. This recommendation remains in place since the 2022/2023 peer review.

Appropriate use of CbC reports

Pakistan confirms that its rules have not changed and continue to be applied effectively. Pakistan continues to meet all terms of reference.

Panama

Overview of CbC reporting requirements

First reporting fiscal year: Commencing on or after 1 January 2018

Consolidated group revenue threshold: EUR 750 million

Filing deadline: 12 months following the end of the reporting fiscal year

Local filing required: No

Surrogate parent entity filing permitted: Yes

First review of the domestic legal framework: 2019/2020

Summary of recommendations

Area of implementation	Recommendations for improvement
Domestic legal and administrative framework	None.
Exchange of information framework	None.
Appropriate use	None.

The domestic legal and administrative framework

Panama confirms that its rules have not changed and continue to be applied effectively. Panama continues to meet all terms of reference.

The exchange of information framework

Panama confirms that its rules have not changed and continue to be applied effectively. Panama continues to meet all terms of reference.

Appropriate use of CbC reports

Panama confirms that its rules have not changed and continue to be applied effectively. Panama continues to meet all terms of reference.

Papua New Guinea

Overview of CbC reporting requirements

First reporting fiscal year: Commencing on or after 1 January 2017

Consolidated group revenue threshold: PGK 2.3 billion

Filing deadline: 12 months following the end of the reporting fiscal year

Local filing required: Requirement suspended

Surrogate parent entity filing permitted: Yes

First review of the domestic legal framework: 2018/2019

Summary of recommendations

Area of implementation	Recommendations for improvement
Domestic legal and administrative framework	It is recommended that Papua New Guinea take steps to amend its legislation or otherwise alter the threshold condition to bring it in line with the Action 13 minimum standard. It is recommended that Papua New Guinea amend its legislation or otherwise take steps to ensure that provisions to enforce the effective implementation of CbC reporting requirements are provided for.
Exchange of information framework	It is recommended that Papua New Guinea take steps to implement processes or written procedures to ensure that the exchange of information is conducted in a manner consistent with the terms of reference relating to the exchange of information framework ahead of the first exchanges of information.
Appropriate use	Not reviewed.

The domestic legal and administrative framework

It is recommended that Papua New Guinea take steps to amend its legislation or otherwise alter the threshold condition to bring it in line with the Action 13 minimum standard. This recommendation remains in place since the 2018/2019 peer review.

It is recommended that Papua New Guinea amend its legislation or otherwise take steps to ensure that provisions to enforce the effective implementation of CbC reporting requirements are provided for. This recommendation remains in place since the 2018/2019 peer review.

The exchange of information framework

It is recommended that Papua New Guinea take steps to implement processes or written procedures to ensure that the exchange of information is conducted in a manner consistent with the terms of reference relating to the exchange of information framework ahead of the first exchanges of information. This recommendation remains in place since the 2018/2019 peer review.

Appropriate use of CbC reports

Papua New Guinea is a non-reciprocal jurisdiction and, as such, will not receive CbC reports submitted to tax authorities in other jurisdictions, and will not apply local filing. It is therefore not necessary for this peer review evaluation to reach any conclusions with respect to Papua New Guinea's compliance with the terms of reference on appropriate use.

For information, Papua New Guinea has provided details of the controls it has in place to ensure the appropriate use of CbC reports, which comply with published Guidance on the Appropriate Use of Information Contained in CbC Reports.

Paraguay

Overview of CbC reporting requirements

Paraguay has not yet introduced a requirement for the filing of CbC reports, as required under the BEPS Action 13 (CbC reporting) minimum standard.

Summary of recommendations

Area of implementation	Recommendations for improvement
Domestic legal and administrative framework	It is recommended that Paraguay take steps to implement a domestic legal and administrative framework to impose and enforce CbC reporting requirements as soon as possible.
Exchange of information framework	It is recommended that Paraguay take steps to have qualifying competent authority agreements in effect with jurisdictions of the Inclusive Framework that meet the confidentiality, consistency and appropriate use conditions and with which Paraguay has an international exchange of information agreement in effect that allows for the automatic exchange of tax information. It is recommended that Paraguay take steps to implement the necessary processes or written procedures to ensure that the exchange of information is conducted in a manner consistent with the terms of reference relating to the exchange of information framework.
Appropriate use	It is recommended that Paraguay take steps to ensure that the appropriate use condition is met ahead of the first exchanges of information.

The domestic legal and administrative framework

Paraguay does not yet have legislation in place to implement the BEPS Action 13 minimum standard.

It is recommended that Paraguay take steps to implement a domestic legal and administrative framework to impose and enforce CbC reporting requirements as soon as possible. This recommendation remains in place since the 2017/2018 peer review.

The exchange of information framework

Paraguay has no bilateral relationships in place for the exchange of CbC reports nor processes to ensure that the exchange of information is conducted in a manner consistent with the terms of reference relating to the exchange of information framework.

It is recommended that Paraguay take steps to have qualifying competent authority agreements in effect with jurisdictions of the Inclusive Framework that meet the confidentiality, consistency and appropriate use conditions and with which Paraguay has an international exchange of information agreement in effect that allows for the automatic exchange of tax information. This recommendation remains in place since the 2017/2018 peer review.

It is recommended that Paraguay take steps to implement the necessary processes or written procedures to ensure that the exchange of information is conducted in a manner consistent with the terms of reference relating to the exchange of information framework. This recommendation remains in place since the 2018/2019 peer review.

Appropriate use of CbC reports

Paraguay does not yet have controls in place to ensure the appropriate use of CbC reports.

It is recommended that Paraguay take steps to ensure that the appropriate use condition is met ahead of the first exchanges of information. This recommendation remains in place since the 2017/2018 peer review.

Peru

Overview of CbC reporting requirements

First reporting fiscal year: Commencing on or after 1 January 2017

Consolidated group revenue threshold: PEN 2.7 billion

Filing deadline: 12 months following the end of the reporting fiscal year

Local filing required: Yes

Surrogate parent entity filing permitted: Yes

First review of the domestic legal framework: 2017/2018

Summary of recommendations

Area of implementation	Recommendations for improvement
Domestic legal and administrative framework	None.
Exchange of information framework	None.
Appropriate use	None.

The domestic legal and administrative framework

Peru confirms that its rules have not changed and continue to be applied effectively. Peru continues to meet all terms of reference.

The exchange of information framework

Peru confirms that its rules have not changed and continue to be applied effectively. Peru continues to meet all terms of reference.

Appropriate use of CbC reports

Peru confirms that its rules have not changed and continue to be applied effectively. Peru continues to meet all terms of reference.

Poland

Overview of CbC reporting requirements

First reporting fiscal year: Commencing on or after 1 January 2016

Consolidated group revenue threshold: EUR 750 million

Filing deadline: 12 months following the end of the reporting fiscal year

Local filing required: Yes, for reporting fiscal years commencing on or after 1 January 2017

Surrogate parent entity filing permitted: Yes

First review of the domestic legal framework: 2017/2018

Summary of recommendations

Area of implementation	Recommendations for improvement
Domestic legal and administrative framework	None.
Exchange of information framework	None.
Appropriate use	None.

The domestic legal and administrative framework

Poland confirms that its rules have not changed and continue to be applied effectively. Poland continues to meet all terms of reference.

The exchange of information framework

Poland made an exchange of CbC reports after the deadline due to a technical issue. This issue has been resolved, and so no recommendation is required.

Poland confirms that its rules have not changed and continue to be applied effectively. Poland continues to meet all terms of reference.

Appropriate use of CbC reports

Poland confirms that its rules have not changed and continue to be applied effectively. Poland continues to meet all terms of reference.

Portugal

Overview of CbC reporting requirements

First reporting fiscal year: Commencing on or after 1 January 2016

Consolidated group revenue threshold: EUR 750 million

Filing deadline: 12 months following the end of the reporting fiscal year

Local filing required: Yes, for reporting fiscal years commencing on or after 1 January 2017

Surrogate parent entity filing permitted: Yes

First review of the domestic legal framework: 2017/2018

Summary of recommendations

Area of implementation	Recommendations for improvement
Domestic legal and administrative framework	None.
Exchange of information framework	None.
Appropriate use	None.

The domestic legal and administrative framework

Portugal confirms that its rules have not changed and continue to be applied effectively. Portugal continues to meet all terms of reference.

The exchange of information framework

Portugal confirms that its rules have not changed and continue to be applied effectively. Portugal continues to meet all terms of reference.

Appropriate use of CbC reports

Portugal confirms that its rules have not changed and continue to be applied effectively. Portugal continues to meet all terms of reference.

Qatar

Overview of CbC reporting requirements

First reporting fiscal year: Commencing on or after 1 January 2018

Consolidated group revenue threshold: QAR 3 billion

Filing deadline: 12 months following the end of the reporting fiscal year

Local filing required: Requirement suspended

Surrogate parent entity filing permitted: Yes

First review of the domestic legal framework: 2017/2018

Summary of recommendations

Area of implementation	Recommendations for improvement
Domestic legal and administrative framework	None.
Exchange of information framework	None.
Appropriate use	Not reviewed.

The domestic legal and administrative framework

Qatar confirms that its rules have not changed and continue to be applied effectively. Qatar continues to meet all terms of reference.

The exchange of information framework

Qatar confirms that its rules have not changed and continue to be applied effectively. Qatar continues to meet all terms of reference.

Appropriate use of CbC reports

Qatar is a non-reciprocal jurisdiction and, as such, will not receive CbC reports submitted to tax authorities in other jurisdictions, and will not apply local filing. It is not necessary for this peer review evaluation to reach any conclusion with respect to Qatar's compliance with the terms of reference on appropriate use.

Romania

Overview of CbC reporting requirements

First reporting fiscal year: Commencing on or after 1 January 2016

Consolidated group revenue threshold: EUR 750 million

Filing deadline: 12 months following the end of the reporting fiscal year

Local filing required: Yes, for reporting fiscal years commencing on or after 1 January 2017

Surrogate parent entity filing permitted: Yes

First review of the domestic legal framework: 2017/2018

Summary of recommendations

Area of implementation	Recommendations for improvement
Domestic legal and administrative framework	It is recommended that Romania take steps to align its local filing implementation with that required by the Action 13 minimum standard.
Exchange of information framework	None.
Appropriate use	Not reviewed.

The domestic legal and administrative framework

It is recommended that Romania take steps to align its local filing implementation with that required by the Action 13 minimum standard. This recommendation remains in place since the 2017/2018 review.

The exchange of information framework

Romania notified some late exchanges of CbC reports, due to a technical issue. This has now been fixed and so no recommendation has been made.

Romania confirms that its rules have not changed and continue to be applied effectively. Romania continues to meet all terms of reference.

Appropriate use of CbC reports

Romania is a non-reciprocal jurisdiction and, as such, will not receive CbC reports submitted to tax authorities in other jurisdictions. It is therefore not necessary for this peer review evaluation to reach any conclusions with respect to Romania's compliance with the terms of reference on appropriate use.

For information, Romania has provided details of the controls it has in place to ensure the appropriate use of CbC reports, which comply with published Guidance on the Appropriate Use of Information Contained in CbC Reports.

Russian Federation

Overview of CbC reporting requirements

First reporting fiscal year: Commencing on or after 1 January 2017

Consolidated group revenue threshold: RUB 50 billion

Filing deadline: 12 months following the end of the reporting fiscal year

Local filing required: Yes

Surrogate parent entity filing permitted: Yes

First review of the domestic legal framework: 2017/2018

Summary of recommendations

Area of implementation	Recommendations for improvement
Domestic legal and administrative framework	It is recommended that Russia amend its legislation or otherwise takes steps to ensure that local filing is only required in the circumstances contained in the terms of reference. It is recommended that Russia amend its legislation or otherwise take steps to ensure that enforcement provisions and monitoring relating to CbC reporting's effective implementation are provided for as contained in the terms of reference as from the first reporting period.
Exchange of information framework	None.
Appropriate use	None.

The domestic legal and administrative framework

It is recommended that Russia amend its legislation or otherwise takes steps to ensure that local filing is only required in the circumstances contained in the terms of reference. This recommendation remains in place since the 2017/2018 peer review.

It is recommended that Russia amend its legislation or otherwise take steps to ensure that enforcement provisions and monitoring relating to CbC reporting's effective implementation are provided for as contained in the terms of reference as from the first reporting period. This recommendation remains in place since the 2017/2018 peer review.

The exchange of information framework

Russia confirms that its rules have not changed and continue to be applied effectively. Russia continues to meet all terms of reference.

Appropriate use of CbC reports

Russia confirms that its rules have not changed and continue to be applied effectively. Russia continues to meet all terms of reference.

Saint Lucia

Overview of CbC reporting requirements

Saint Lucia has not yet introduced a requirement for the filing of CbC reports, as required under the BEPS Action 13 (CbC reporting) minimum standard.

Summary of recommendations

Area of implementation	Recommendations for improvement
Domestic legal and administrative framework	It is recommended that Saint Lucia take steps to implement a domestic legal and administrative framework to impose and enforce CbC reporting requirements as soon as possible.
Exchange of information framework	It is recommended that Saint Lucia take steps to have qualifying competent authority agreements in effect with jurisdictions of the Inclusive Framework that meet the confidentiality, consistency and appropriate use conditions and with which Saint Lucia has an international exchange of information agreement in effect that allows for the automatic exchange of tax information. It is recommended that Saint Lucia take steps to implement the necessary processes or written procedures to ensure that the exchange of information is conducted in a manner consistent with the terms of reference relating to the exchange of information framework.
Appropriate use	It is recommended that Saint Lucia take steps to ensure that the appropriate use condition is met ahead of the first exchanges of information.

The domestic legal and administrative framework

Saint Lucia does not yet have legislation in place to implement the BEPS Action 13 minimum standard.

It is recommended that Saint Lucia take steps to implement a domestic legal and administrative framework to impose and enforce CbC reporting requirements as soon as possible. This recommendation remains in place since the 2018/2019 peer review.

The exchange of information framework

Saint Lucia has no bilateral relationships in place for the exchange of CbC reports nor processes to ensure that the exchange of information is conducted in a manner consistent with the terms of reference relating to the exchange of information framework.

It is recommended that Saint Lucia take steps to have qualifying competent authority agreements in effect with jurisdictions of the Inclusive Framework that meet the confidentiality, consistency and appropriate use conditions and with which Saint Lucia has an international exchange of information agreement in effect that allows for the automatic exchange of tax information. This recommendation remains in place since the 2018/2019 peer review.

It is recommended that Saint Lucia take steps to implement the necessary processes or written procedures to ensure that the exchange of information is conducted in a manner consistent with the terms of reference relating to the exchange of information framework. This recommendation remains in place since the 2018/2019 peer review.

Appropriate use of CbC reports

Saint Lucia does not yet have controls in place to ensure the appropriate use of CbC reports.

It is recommended that Saint Lucia take steps to ensure that the appropriate use condition is met ahead of the first exchanges of information. This recommendation remains in place since the 2018/2019 peer review.

Saint Vincent and the Grenadines

Overview of CbC reporting requirements

Saint Vincent and the Grenadines has not yet introduced a requirement for the filing of CbC reports, as required under the BEPS Action 13 (CbC reporting) minimum standard.

Summary of recommendations

Area of implementation	Recommendations for improvement
Domestic legal and administrative framework	It is recommended that Saint Vincent and the Grenadines take steps to implement a domestic legal and administrative framework to impose and enforce CbC reporting requirements as soon as possible.
Exchange of information framework	It is recommended that Saint Vincent and the Grenadines take steps to have qualifying competent authority agreements in effect with jurisdictions of the Inclusive Framework that meet the confidentiality, consistency and appropriate use conditions and with which Saint Vincent and the Grenadines has an international exchange of information agreement in effect that allows for the automatic exchange of tax information. It is recommended that Saint Vincent and the Grenadines take steps to implement the necessary processes or written procedures to ensure that the exchange of information is conducted in a manner consistent with the terms of reference relating to the exchange of information framework.
Appropriate use	It is recommended that Saint Vincent and the Grenadines take steps to ensure that the appropriate use condition is met ahead of the first exchanges of information.

The domestic legal and administrative framework

Saint Vincent and the Grenadines does not yet have legislation in place to implement the BEPS Action 13 minimum standard.

It is recommended that Saint Vincent and the Grenadines take steps to implement a domestic legal and administrative framework to impose and enforce CbC reporting requirements as soon as possible. This recommendation remains in place since the 2019/2020 peer review.

The exchange of information framework

Saint Vincent and the Grenadines has no bilateral relationships in place for the exchange of CbC reports nor processes to ensure that the exchange of information is conducted in a manner consistent with the terms of reference relating to the exchange of information framework.

It is recommended that Saint Vincent and the Grenadines take steps to have qualifying competent authority agreements in effect with jurisdictions of the Inclusive Framework that meet the confidentiality, consistency and appropriate use conditions and with which Saint Vincent and the Grenadines has an international exchange of information agreement in effect that allows for the automatic exchange of tax information. This recommendation remains in place since the 2019/2020 peer review.

It is recommended that Saint Vincent and the Grenadines take steps to implement the necessary processes or written procedures to ensure that the exchange of information is conducted in a manner consistent with the terms of reference relating to the exchange of information framework. This recommendation remains in place since the 2019/2020 peer review.

Appropriate use of CbC reports

Saint Vincent and the Grenadines does not yet have controls in place to ensure the appropriate use of CbC reports.

It is recommended that Saint Vincent and the Grenadines take steps to ensure that the appropriate use condition is met ahead of the first exchanges of information. This recommendation remains in place since the 2019/2020 peer review.

San Marino

Overview of CbC reporting requirements

First reporting fiscal year: Commencing on or after 1 January 2019

Consolidated group revenue threshold: EUR 750 million

Filing deadline: 12 months following the end of the reporting fiscal year

Local filing required: Yes

Surrogate parent entity filing permitted: Yes

First review of the domestic legal framework: 2018/2019

Summary of recommendations

Area of implementation	Recommendations for improvement
Domestic legal and administrative framework	None.
Exchange of information framework	None.
Appropriate use	None.

The domestic legal and administrative framework

San Marino has introduced an administrative sanction which applies in cases where a resident constituent entity fails to notify the San Marino Tax Office that it belongs to an MNE Group above the consolidated group revenue threshold by the required date.[1]

San Marino confirms that its rules have not changed and continue to be applied effectively. San Marino continues to meet all terms of reference.

The exchange of information framework

San Marino confirms that its rules have not changed and continue to be applied effectively. San Marino continues to meet all terms of reference.

Appropriate use of CbC reports

San Marino confirms that its rules have not changed and continue to be applied effectively. San Marino continues to meet all terms of reference.

Note

[1] https://www.bollettinoufficiale.sm/on-line/RicercaBU?operation=getDocumentiFisici&id=11c536df38cf3bde3af930c725c63cc930fa27c525cf27de3ccf26fe2cda30f5339f37cc6dcc369b789f66ce6287649b30cf78cb609c668763c8369a3693379c369f609e758a758a758a758a758a758a758a758a758a758a758a758a758a758a758a758a758a758a758a758a758a758a758a758a758a758a758a758a758a&position=0

Saudi Arabia

Overview of CbC reporting requirements

First reporting fiscal year: Commencing on or after 1 January 2018

Consolidated group revenue threshold: SAR 3.2 billion

Filing deadline: 12 months following the end of the reporting fiscal year

Local filing required: Yes

Surrogate parent entity filing permitted: Yes

First review of the domestic legal framework: 2019/2020

Summary of recommendations

Area of implementation	Recommendations for improvement
Domestic legal and administrative framework	None.
Exchange of information framework	None.
Appropriate use	None.

The domestic legal and administrative framework

Saudi Arabia confirms that its rules have not changed and continue to be applied effectively. Saudi Arabia continues to meet all terms of reference

The exchange of information framework

Saudi Arabia confirms that its rules have not changed and continue to be applied effectively. Saudi Arabia continues to meet all terms of reference

Appropriate use of CbC reports

Saudi Arabia confirms that its rules have not changed and continue to be applied effectively. Saudi Arabia continues to meet all terms of reference.

Senegal

Overview of CbC reporting requirements

First reporting fiscal year: Commencing on or after 1 January 2018

Consolidated group revenue threshold: XOF 492 billion

Filing deadline: 12 months following the end of the reporting fiscal year

Local filing required: Yes

Surrogate parent entity filing permitted: Yes

First review of the domestic legal framework: 2018/2019

Summary of recommendations

Area of implementation	Recommendations for improvement
Domestic legal and administrative framework	It is recommended that Senegal complete the definition of an "Ultimate Parent Entity" in a manner that is consistent with the terms of reference. It is recommended that Senegal amend or otherwise clarify the annual consolidated revenue threshold calculation rule in respect of MNE Groups whose Ultimate Parent Entity is located in a jurisdiction other than Senegal which may deviate from the guidance issued by the OECD. It is recommended that Senegal amend the conditions for local filing or otherwise take steps to ensure that local filing can only be required in the circumstances contained in the terms of reference.
Exchange of information framework	It is recommended that Senegal take steps to have qualifying competent authority agreements in effect with jurisdictions of the Inclusive Framework which meet the confidentiality, consistency and appropriate use conditions and with which Senegal has an international exchange of information agreement in effect that allows for the automatic exchange of tax information. It is recommended that Senegal have in place the necessary processes or written procedures to ensure that the exchange of information is conducted in a manner consistent with the terms of reference relating to the exchange of information framework.
Appropriate use	It is recommended that Senegal take steps to ensure that the appropriate use condition is met ahead of the first exchanges of information.

The domestic legal and administrative framework

Senegal has the following recommendations relating to its domestic legal and administrative framework. These recommendations remain in place since the 2018/2019 peer report.[1 2]

The definition of Ultimate Parent Entity

Senegal's legislation does not include a complete definition of "Ultimate Parent Entity". It is recommended that Senegal amend the definition of UPE or otherwise clarify the definition to be in line with the standard.

The definition of Group

Senegal's 2018/2019 peer review report included a recommendation that Senegal amend its legislation to include a definition of "Group" that is in line with the standard. Senegal has amended its legislation and this recommendation is removed.

The definition of MNE Group

Senegal's 2018/2019 peer review report included a recommendation that Senegal amend its legislation to include a definition of "MNE Group" that is in line with the standard. Senegal has amended its legislation and this recommendation is removed.

The definition of Constituent Entity

Senegal's 2018/2019 peer review report included a recommendation that Senegal amend its legislation to include a definition of "Constituent Entity" that is in line with the standard. Senegal has amended its legislation and this recommendation is removed.

Contents of the Country-by-Country report

Senegal's 2018/2019 peer review report included a recommendation that Senegal publish the full content and format requirements of the CbC Report. Senegal has published the full content and format requirements of the CbC Report and this recommendation is removed.

The local filing provision

Senegal has a legislative requirement which is in effect despite Senegal not yet meeting all of the consistency, confidentiality and appropriate use conditions. It is therefore recommended that Senegal take steps to ensure that local filing only occurs in the circumstances permitted under the minimum standard.

Currency Fluctuations

It is recommended that Senegal clarify that the annual consolidated group revenue threshold calculation rule applies in line with the OECD guidance on currency fluctuations in respect of an MNE Group whose Ultimate Parent Entity is located in a jurisdiction other than Senegal.

Effective implementation

Senegal's 2017/2018 peer review report included a recommendation to take steps to have enforcement measures in place in case of incomplete or erroneous filing. Senegal has amended its legislation and this recommendation is removed.[3]

The exchange of information framework

Senegal has no bilateral relationships in place for the exchange of CbC reports nor processes to ensure that the exchange of information is conducted in a manner consistent with the terms of reference relating to the exchange of information framework.

It is recommended that Senegal take steps to have qualifying competent authority agreements in effect with jurisdictions of the Inclusive Framework which meet the confidentiality, consistency and appropriate use conditions and with which Senegal has an international exchange of information agreement in effect that allows for the automatic exchange of tax information. This recommendation remains in place since the 2017/2018 peer review.

It is recommended that Senegal have in place the necessary processes or written procedures to ensure that the exchange of information is conducted in a manner consistent with the terms of reference relating to the exchange of information framework. This recommendation remains in place since the 2018/2019 peer review.

Appropriate use of CbC reports

Senegal does not yet have controls in place to ensure the appropriate use of CbC reports. It is recommended that Senegal take steps to ensure that the appropriate use condition is met ahead of the first exchanges of information. This recommendation remains in place since the 2017/2018 peer review.

Notes

[1] Senegal's local filing requirements will not apply if there is surrogate filing in another jurisdiction which is listed in a list of states or territories which have adopted regulations imposing the filing of a CbC report similar to that required in Senegal, which have concluded an agreement with Senegal for the automatic exchange of CbC reports and which comply with the obligations arising from such agreement. It is unclear whether local filing would be "deactivated" in respect of jurisdictions which allow voluntary parent surrogate filing, being noted that the list mentioned above has not yet been published at this point in time. A monitoring point on this remains in place since the 2018/2019 peer review.

[2] There are no specific processes in place that would allow Senegal to take appropriate measures in case it is notified by another jurisdiction that such other jurisdiction has reason to believe that an error may have led to incorrect or incomplete information reporting by a Reporting Entity or that there is non-compliance of a Reporting Entity with respect to its obligation to file a CbC report. As no exchange of CbC reports has yet occurred, this aspect is being monitored. This monitoring point remains in place since the 2018/2019 peer review.

[3] https://budget.sec.gouv.sn/telecharger-le-document/65a7055d-e038-4c83-a5f2-46870a2a028a/telechargement

Serbia

Overview of CbC reporting requirements

First reporting fiscal year: Commencing on or after 1 January 2020

Consolidated group revenue threshold: EUR 750 million

Filing deadline: 12 months following the end of the reporting fiscal year

Local filing required: No

Surrogate parent entity filing permitted: No

First review of the domestic legal framework: 2020/2021

Summary of recommendations

Area of implementation	Recommendations for improvement
Domestic legal and administrative framework	None.
Exchange of information framework	It is recommended that Serbia take steps to have qualifying competent authority agreements in effect with jurisdictions of the Inclusive Framework that meet the confidentiality, consistency and appropriate use conditions and with which Serbia has an international exchange of information agreement in effect that allows for the automatic exchange of tax information. It is recommended that Serbia take steps to implement the necessary processes or written procedures to ensure that the exchange of information is conducted in a manner consistent with the terms of reference relating to the exchange of information framework.
Appropriate use	It is recommended that Serbia take steps to ensure that the appropriate use condition is met ahead of the first exchanges of information.

The domestic legal and administrative framework

Serbia confirms that its rules have not changed and continue to be applied effectively. Serbia continues to meet all terms of reference.

The exchange of information framework

Serbia has no bilateral relationships in place for the exchange of CbC reports nor processes to ensure that the exchange of information is conducted in a manner consistent with the terms of reference relating to the exchange of information framework.

It is recommended that Serbia take steps to have qualifying competent authority agreements in effect with jurisdictions of the Inclusive Framework that meet the confidentiality, consistency and appropriate use conditions and with which Serbia has an international exchange of information agreement in effect that allows for the automatic exchange of tax information. This recommendation remains in place since the 2018/2019 peer review.

It is recommended that Serbia take steps to implement the necessary processes or written procedures to ensure that the exchange of information is conducted in a manner consistent with the terms of reference relating to the exchange of information framework. This recommendation remains in place since the 2018/2019 peer review.

Appropriate use of CbC reports

Serbia does not yet have controls in place to ensure the appropriate use of CbC reports.

It is recommended that Serbia take steps to ensure that the appropriate use condition is met ahead of the first exchanges of information. This recommendation remains in place since the 2018/2019 peer review.

Seychelles

Overview of CbC reporting requirements

First reporting fiscal year: Commencing on or after 1 January 2018.

Consolidated group revenue threshold: EUR 750 million

Filing deadline: 12 months following the end of the reporting fiscal year

Local filing required: No

Surrogate parent entity filing permitted: No

First review of the domestic legal framework: 2017/2018

Summary of recommendations

Area of implementation	Recommendations for improvement
Domestic legal and administrative framework	None
Exchange of information framework	None.
Appropriate use	None.

The domestic legal and administrative framework

Seychelles confirms that its rules have not changed and continue to be applied effectively. Seychelles continues to meet all terms of reference.

The exchange of information framework

Seychelles 2018/2019 peer review included a recommendation that Seychelles take steps to implement processes or written procedures to ensure that the exchange of information is conducted in a manner consistent with the terms of reference relating to the exchange of information framework as soon as possible. These processes are now in place and the recommendation is removed.

Appropriate use of CbC reports

Seychelles 2017/2018 peer review included a recommendation that Seychelles take steps to ensure that the appropriate use condition is met as soon as possible. These processes are now in place and the recommendation is removed.

Seychelles meets all terms of reference with respect to the appropriate use condition.

Sierra Leone

Overview of CbC reporting requirements

Sierra Leone has not yet introduced a requirement for the filing of CbC reports, as required under the BEPS Action 13 (CbC reporting) minimum standard.

Summary of recommendations

Area of implementation	Recommendations for improvement
Domestic legal and administrative framework	It is recommended that Sierra Leone take steps to implement a domestic legal and administrative framework to impose and enforce CbC reporting requirements as soon as possible.
Exchange of information framework	It is recommended that Sierra Leone take steps to have qualifying competent authority agreements in effect with jurisdictions of the Inclusive Framework that meet the confidentiality, consistency and appropriate use conditions and with which Sierra Leone has an international exchange of information agreement in effect that allows for the automatic exchange of tax information. It is recommended that Sierra Leone take steps to implement the necessary processes or written procedures to ensure that the exchange of information is conducted in a manner consistent with the terms of reference relating to the exchange of information framework.
Appropriate use	It is recommended that Sierra Leone take steps to ensure that the appropriate use condition is met ahead of the first exchanges of information.

The domestic legal and administrative framework

Sierra Leone does not yet have legislation in place to implement the BEPS Action 13 minimum standard.

It is recommended that Sierra Leone take steps to implement a domestic legal and administrative framework to impose and enforce CbC reporting requirements as soon as possible. This recommendation remains in place since the 2018/2019 peer review.

The exchange of information framework

Sierra Leone has no bilateral relationships in place for the exchange of CbC reports nor processes to ensure that the exchange of information is conducted in a manner consistent with the terms of reference relating to the exchange of information framework.

It is recommended that Sierra Leone take steps to have qualifying competent authority agreements in effect with jurisdictions of the Inclusive Framework that meet the confidentiality, consistency and appropriate use conditions and with which Sierra Leone has an international exchange of information agreement in effect that allows for the automatic exchange of tax information. This recommendation remains in place since the 2018/2019 peer review.

It is recommended that Sierra Leone take steps to implement the necessary processes or written procedures to ensure that the exchange of information is conducted in a manner consistent with the terms of reference relating to the exchange of information framework. This recommendation remains in place since the 2018/2019 peer review.

Appropriate use of CbC reports

Sierra Leone does not yet have controls in place to ensure the appropriate use of CbC reports.

It is recommended that Sierra Leone take steps to ensure that the appropriate use condition is met ahead of the first exchanges of information. This recommendation remains in place since the 2018/2019 peer review.

Singapore

Overview of CbC reporting requirements

First reporting fiscal year: Commencing on or after 1 January 2017. Singapore also allowed MNE Groups to file a CbC report on a voluntary basis, for reporting fiscal years commencing between 1 January 2016 and 31 December 2016.

Consolidated group revenue threshold: SGD 1.125 billion

Filing deadline: 12 months following the end of the reporting fiscal year

Local filing required: No

Surrogate parent entity filing permitted: Yes

First review of the domestic legal framework: 2017/2018

Summary of recommendations

Area of implementation	Recommendations for improvement
Domestic legal and administrative framework	None.
Exchange of information framework	None.
Appropriate use	None.

The domestic legal and administrative framework

Singapore confirms that its rules have not changed and continue to be applied effectively. Singapore continues to meet all terms of reference.[1] [2] [3] [4]

The exchange of information framework

Singapore confirms that its rules have not changed and continue to be applied effectively. Singapore continues to meet all terms of reference.

Appropriate use of CbC reports

Singapore confirms that its rules have not changed and continue to be applied effectively. Singapore continues to meet all terms of reference.

Notes

[1] Singapore's 2017/2018 peer review included a monitoring point in relation to a "designation provision". This monitoring point remains in place.

[2] Singapore's 2017/2018 peer review included a monitoring point in relation to the ability of the Comptroller to allow a CbC report to be filed later than the filing deadline as set in the regulations. This monitoring point remains in place.

[3] Singapore's 2017/2018 peer review included a monitoring point whereby if local filing requirements were introduced, these requirements should comply with the terms of reference under paragraph 8 (c). This monitoring point remains in place.

[4] Singapore's 2017/2018 peer review included a monitoring point whereby if local filing requirements were introduced, these requirements should be deactivated in case of surrogate filing in a manner consistent with the terms of reference under paragraph 8 (d). This monitoring point remains in place.

Slovak Republic

Overview of CbC reporting requirements

First reporting fiscal year: Commencing on or after 1 January 2016

Consolidated group revenue threshold: EUR 750 million

Filing deadline: 12 months following the end of the reporting fiscal year

Local filing required: Yes, for reporting fiscal years commencing on or after 1 January 2017

Surrogate parent entity filing permitted: Yes

First review of the domestic legal framework: 2017/2018

Summary of recommendations

Area of implementation	Recommendations for improvement
Domestic legal and administrative framework	None.
Exchange of information framework	None.
Appropriate use	None.

The domestic legal and administrative framework

The Slovak Republic confirms that its rules have not changed and continue to be applied effectively. The Slovak Republic continues to meet all terms of reference.

The exchange of information framework

The Slovak Republic confirms that its rules have not changed and continue to be applied effectively. The Slovak Republic continues to meet all terms of reference.

Appropriate use of CbC reports

The Slovak Republic confirms that its rules have not changed and continue to be applied effectively. The Slovak Republic continues to meet all terms of reference.

Slovenia

Overview of CbC reporting requirements

First reporting fiscal year: Commencing on or after 1 January 2016

Consolidated group revenue threshold: EUR 750 million

Filing deadline: 12 months following the end of the reporting fiscal year

Local filing required: Yes, for reporting fiscal years commencing on or after 1 January 2017

Surrogate parent entity filing permitted: Yes

First review of the domestic legal framework: 2017/2018

Summary of recommendations

Area of implementation	Recommendations for improvement
Domestic legal and administrative framework	None.
Exchange of information framework	None.
Appropriate use	None.

The domestic legal and administrative framework

Slovenia confirms that its rules have not changed and continue to be applied effectively. Slovenia continues to meet all terms of reference.[1]

The exchange of information framework

Slovenia confirms that its rules have not changed and continue to be applied effectively. Slovenia continues to meet all terms of reference.

Appropriate use of CbC reports

Slovenia confirms that its rules have not changed and continue to be applied effectively. Slovenia continues to meet all terms of reference.

Note

[1] Slovenia's 2017/2018 peer review included a general monitoring point relating to a specific process to that would allow to take appropriate measures in case Slovenia is notified by another jurisdiction that such

other jurisdiction has reason to believe that an error may have led to incorrect or incomplete information reporting by a Reporting Entity or that there is non-compliance of a Reporting Entity with respect to its obligation to file a CbC report. This monitoring point remains in place.

South Africa

Overview of CbC reporting requirements

First reporting fiscal year: Commencing on or after 1 January 2016

Consolidated group revenue threshold: ZAR 10 billion

Filing deadline: 12 months following the end of the reporting fiscal year

Local filing required: Yes

Surrogate parent entity filing permitted: No

First review of the domestic legal framework: 2017/2018

Summary of recommendations

Area of implementation	Recommendations for improvement
Domestic legal and administrative framework	None.
Exchange of information framework	None.
Appropriate use	None.

The domestic legal and administrative framework

South Africa confirms that its rules have not changed and continue to be applied effectively. South Africa continues to meet all terms of reference.

The exchange of information framework

South Africa confirms that its rules have not changed and continue to be applied effectively. South Africa continues to meet all terms of reference.

Appropriate use of CbC reports

South Africa confirms that its rules have not changed and continue to be applied effectively. South Africa continues to meet all terms of reference.

Spain

Overview of CbC reporting requirements

First reporting fiscal year: Commencing on or after 1 January 2016

Consolidated group revenue threshold: EUR 750 million

Filing deadline: 12 months following the end of the reporting fiscal year

Local filing required: Yes

Surrogate parent entity filing permitted: Yes

First review of the domestic legal framework: 2017/2018

Summary of recommendations

Area of implementation	Recommendations for improvement
Domestic legal and administrative framework	None.
Exchange of information framework	None.
Appropriate use	None.

The domestic legal and administrative framework

Spain confirms that its rules have not changed and continue to be applied effectively. Spain continues to meet all terms of reference.[1] [2]

The exchange of information framework

Spain confirms that its rules have not changed and continue to be applied effectively. Spain continues to meet all terms of reference.

Appropriate use of CbC reports

Spain confirms that its rules have not changed and continue to be applied effectively. Spain continues to meet all terms of reference.

Notes

[1] Spain's 2017/2018 peer review included a monitoring point on the potential exclusion of companies which are not required to produce consolidated financial statements from the filing requirement with respect to

the absence in the definition of a "dominant company" of the “deemed listing provision”. This monitoring point remains in place.

[2] Spain’s 2017/2018 peer review included a monitoring point with respect to the absence of a provision relating to the “Source of data” to complete a CbC report. This monitoring point remains in place.

Sri Lanka

Overview of CbC reporting requirements

First reporting fiscal year: Commencing on or after 1 April 2019

Consolidated group revenue threshold: EUR 750 million or its equivalent in LKR

Filing deadline: 12 months following the end of the reporting fiscal year

Local filing required: Yes

Surrogate parent entity filing permitted: Yes

First review of the domestic legal framework: 2018/2019

Summary of recommendations

Area of implementation	Recommendations for improvement
Domestic legal and administrative framework	It is recommended that Sri Lanka amend or otherwise clarify the annual consolidated group revenue threshold calculation rule applies in a manner consistent with the OECD guidance on currency fluctuations in respect of an MNE Group whose Ultimate Parent entity is located in a jurisdiction other than Sri Lanka. It is recommended that Sri Lanka take steps to change its legislation or issue guidance to suspend local filing until they have met the necessary conditions to apply such rules.
Exchange of information framework	It is recommended that Sri Lanka take steps to have qualifying competent authority agreements in effect with jurisdictions of the Inclusive Framework which meet the confidentiality, consistency and appropriate use conditions and with which it has an international exchange of information agreement in effect that allows for the automatic exchange of tax information. It is recommended that Sri Lanka take steps to implement the necessary processes or written procedures to ensure that the exchange of information is conducted in a manner consistent with the terms of reference relating to the exchange of information framework.
Appropriate use	It is recommended that Sri Lanka take steps to ensure that the appropriate use condition is met ahead of the first exchanges of information.

The domestic legal and administrative framework

It is recommended that Sri Lanka amend or otherwise clarify the annual consolidated group revenue threshold calculation rule applies in a manner consistent with the OECD guidance on currency fluctuations in respect of an MNE Group whose Ultimate Parent entity is located in a jurisdiction other than Sri Lanka. This recommendation remains in place since the 2018/2019 peer review.

It is recommended that Sri Lanka take steps to change its legislation or issue guidance to suspend local filing until they have met the necessary conditions to apply such rules. This recommendation remains in place since the 2018/2019 peer review.[1]

The exchange of information framework

Sri Lanka has no bilateral relationships in place for the exchange of CbC reports nor processes to ensure that the exchange of information is conducted in a manner consistent with the terms of reference relating to the exchange of information framework.

It is recommended that Sri Lanka take steps to have qualifying competent authority agreements in effect with jurisdictions of the Inclusive Framework which meet the confidentiality, consistency and appropriate use conditions and with which it has an international exchange of information agreement in effect that allows for the automatic exchange of tax information. This recommendation remains in place since the 2018/2019 peer review.

It is recommended that Sri Lanka take steps to implement the necessary processes or written procedures to ensure that the exchange of information is conducted in a manner consistent with the terms of reference relating to the exchange of information framework. This recommendation remains in place since the 2018/2019 peer review.

Appropriate use of CbC reports

Sri Lanka does not yet have controls in place to ensure the appropriate use of CbC reports.

It is recommended that Sri Lanka take steps to ensure that the appropriate use condition is met ahead of the first exchanges of information. This recommendation remains in place since the 2018/2019 peer review.

Note

[1] Sri Lanka's Regulations on Transfer Pricing refer to the responsibility to prepare and maintain transfer pricing documentation including the Country-by-Country Report applying to enterprises carrying out controlled transactions with associated enterprises subject to sections of Sri Lanka's primary legislation. This narrows the population of MNEs required to file a CbC report in Sri Lanka and apparently applies an exemption from reporting to MNEs who meet the threshold requirement but do not carry out controlled transactions with associated enterprises. In practice this is very unlikely to be the case for MNEs who would otherwise meet the requirement so no recommendation is made but the situation will be monitored. This monitoring point remains in place since the 2018/2019 peer review.

Sweden

Overview of CbC reporting requirements

First reporting fiscal year: Commencing on or after 1 January 2016

Consolidated group revenue threshold: SEK 7 billion

Filing deadline: 12 months following the end of the reporting fiscal year

Local filing required: Yes

Surrogate parent entity filing permitted: Yes

First review of the domestic legal framework: 2017/2018

Summary of recommendations

Area of implementation	Recommendations for improvement
Domestic legal and administrative framework	None.
Exchange of information framework	None.
Appropriate use	None.

The domestic legal and administrative framework

Sweden confirms that its rules have not changed and continue to be applied effectively. Sweden continues to meet all terms of reference.[1]

The exchange of information framework

Sweden confirms that its rules have not changed and continue to be applied effectively. Sweden continues to meet all terms of reference.

Appropriate use of CbC reports

Sweden confirms that its rules have not changed and continue to be applied effectively. Sweden continues to meet all terms of reference.

Note

[1] Sweden's 2017/2018 peer review included a monitoring point relating to the conditions under which local filing may be required (paragraph 8 (c) iv. b) of the terms of reference). This monitoring point remains in place.

Switzerland

Overview of CbC reporting requirements

First reporting fiscal year: Commencing on or after 1 January 2018. Switzerland also allowed MNE Groups to file a CbC report on a voluntary basis, for reporting fiscal years commencing between 1 January 2016 and 31 December 2017.

Consolidated group revenue threshold: CHF 900 million

Filing deadline: 12 months following the end of the reporting fiscal year

Local filing required: Yes

Surrogate parent entity filing permitted: Yes

First review of the domestic legal framework: 2017/2018

Summary of recommendations

Area of implementation	Recommendations for improvement
Domestic legal and administrative framework	None.
Exchange of information framework	None.
Appropriate use	None.

The domestic legal and administrative framework

Switzerland confirms that its rules have not changed and continue to be applied effectively. Switzerland continues to meet all terms of reference.

The exchange of information framework

Switzerland confirms that its rules have not changed and continue to be applied effectively. Switzerland continues to meet all terms of reference.

Appropriate use of CbC reports

Switzerland confirms that its rules have not changed and continue to be applied effectively. Switzerland continues to meet all terms of reference.

Thailand

Overview of CbC reporting requirements

First reporting fiscal year: Commencing on or after 1 January 2021

Consolidated group revenue threshold: THB 28 billion

Filing deadline: 12 months following the end of the reporting fiscal year

Local filing required: Requirement suspended

Surrogate parent entity filing permitted: Yes

First review of the domestic legal framework: 2021/2022

Summary of recommendations

Area of implementation	Recommendations for improvement
Domestic legal and administrative framework	None.
Exchange of information framework	None.
Appropriate use	None.

The domestic legal and administrative framework

Thailand confirms that its rules have not changed and continue to be applied effectively. Thailand continues to meet all terms of reference.

The exchange of information framework

Thailand notified some late exchanges of CbC reports, due to a technical issue with its exchange of information portal. This has now been fixed and so no recommendation has been made.

Thailand confirms that its rules have not changed and continue to be applied effectively. Thailand continues to meet all terms of reference.

Appropriate use of CbC reports

Thailand confirms that its rules have not changed and continue to be applied effectively. Thailand continues to meet all terms of reference.

Togo

Overview of CbC reporting requirements

First reporting fiscal year: Commencing on or after 1 January 2023

Consolidated group revenue threshold: XOF 492 billion

Filing deadline: 12 months following the end of the reporting fiscal year

Local filing required: Yes

Surrogate parent entity filing permitted: Yes

First review of the domestic legal framework: 2022/2023

Summary of recommendations

Area of implementation	Recommendations for improvement
Domestic legal and administrative framework	It is recommended that Togo introduce or complete the definitions of a "Group", "MNE Group", "Constituent Entity", "Consolidated Financial Statements", "Fiscal Year", "Reporting Fiscal Year", "Reporting Entity", and "Systemic Failure" in a manner that is consistent with the standard.
	It is recommended that Togo publish the full content and format requirements of the CbC Report.
	It is recommended that Togo take steps to ensure that local filing only occurs in the circumstances permitted under the minimum standard.
	It is recommended that Togo clarify that the annual consolidated group revenue threshold calculation rule applies in line with the OECD guidance on currency fluctuations in respect of an MNE Group whose Ultimate Parent Entity is located in a jurisdiction other than Togo.
Exchange of information framework	It is recommended that Togo take steps to have qualifying competent authority agreements in effect with jurisdictions of the Inclusive Framework that meet the confidentiality, consistency and appropriate use conditions and with which Togo has an international exchange of information agreement in effect that allows for the automatic exchange of tax information.
	It is recommended that Togo take steps to implement the necessary processes or written procedures to ensure that the exchange of information is conducted in a manner consistent with the terms of reference relating to the exchange of information framework.
Appropriate use	It is recommended that Togo take steps to ensure that the appropriate use condition is met ahead of the first exchanges of information.

The domestic legal and administrative framework

Togo has a number of recommendations to improve the legislation. These recommendations remain in place since the 2022/2023 peer review.

The definition of Group

Togo's legislation does not include a definition of "Group". It is recommended that Togo amend its legislation to include a definition of "Group" that is in line with the standard.

The definition of MNE Group

Togo's legislation does not include a definition of "MNE Group". It is recommended that Togo amend its legislation to include a definition of "MNE Group" that is in line with the standard.

The definition of Constituent Entity

Togo's legislation does not include a definition of "Constituent Entity". It is recommended that Togo amend its legislation to include a definition of "Constituent Entity" that is in line with the standard.

The definition of Consolidated Financial Statements

Togo's legislation does not include a definition of "Consolidated Financial Statements". It is recommended that Togo amend its legislation to include a definition of "Consolidated Financial Statements" that is in line with the standard.

The definition of Fiscal Year

Togo's legislation does not include a definition of "Fiscal Year". It is recommended that Togo amend its legislation to include a definition of "Fiscal Year" that is in line with the standard.

The definition of Reporting Fiscal Year

Togo's legislation does not include a definition of "Reporting Fiscal Year". It is recommended that Togo amend its legislation to include a definition of "Reporting Fiscal Year" that is in line with the standard.

The definition of Reporting Entity

Togo's legislation does not include a definition of "Reporting Entity". It is recommended that Togo amend its legislation to include a definition of "Reporting Entity" that is in line with the standard.

The definition of Systemic Failure

Togo's legislation does not include a definition of "Systemic Failure". It is recommended that Togo amend its legislation to include a definition of "Systemic Failure" that is in line with the standard.

Contents of the Country-by-Country report

The information included in Togo's legislation does not include the template of the Country-by-Country report and does not include any details of what should be included under each heading in the report. It is recommended that Togo publish the full content and format requirements of the CbC Report.

The local filing provision

Togo has a legislative requirement for local filing which is in effect despite Togo not yet meeting all of the consistency, confidentiality and appropriate use conditions. It is therefore recommended that Togo take steps to ensure that local filing only occurs in the circumstances permitted under the minimum standard.

Currency fluctuations

Where an MNE Group draws up, or would draw up, its Consolidated Financial Statements in a currency other than that specified by Togo, the reference to Togo's threshold has the effect as if it were a reference to the equivalent in that currency at the average exchange rate for the accounting period. While this provision would not create an issue for MNE Groups whose Ultimate Parent Entity is a tax resident in Togo, it may be incompatible with the guidance on currency fluctuations for MNE Groups whose Ultimate Parent Entity is located in another jurisdiction, if local filing requirements were applied in respect of a Constituent Entity (which is a Togolese tax resident) of an MNE Group which does not reach the threshold as determined in the jurisdiction of the Ultimate Parent Entity of such a Group. It is recommended that Togo clarify that the annual consolidated group revenue threshold calculation rule applies in line with the OECD guidance on currency fluctuations in respect of an MNE Group whose Ultimate Parent Entity is located in a jurisdiction other than Togo.

The exchange of information framework

Togo has no bilateral relationships in place for the exchange of CbC reports nor processes to ensure that the exchange of information is conducted in a manner consistent with the terms of reference relating to the exchange of information framework.

It is recommended that Togo take steps to have qualifying competent authority agreements in effect with jurisdictions of the Inclusive Framework that meet the confidentiality, consistency and appropriate use conditions and with which Togo has an international exchange of information agreement in effect that allows for the automatic exchange of tax information. This recommendation remains in place since the 2021/2022 peer review.

It is recommended that Togo take steps to implement the necessary processes or written procedures to ensure that the exchange of information is conducted in a manner consistent with the terms of reference relating to the exchange of information framework. This recommendation remains in place since the 2021/2022 peer review.

Appropriate use of CbC reports

Togo does not yet have controls in place to ensure the appropriate use of CbC reports.

It is recommended that Togo take steps to ensure that the appropriate use condition is met ahead of the first exchanges of information. This recommendation remains in place since the 2021/2022 peer review.

Trinidad and Tobago

Overview of CbC reporting requirements

First reporting fiscal year: To be confirmed

Consolidated group revenue threshold: USD 850 million

Filing deadline: 12 months following the end of the reporting fiscal year

Local filing required: Yes

Surrogate parent entity filing permitted: Yes

First review of domestic legal framework: 2023/2024

Summary of recommendations

Area of implementation	Recommendations for improvement
Domestic legal and administrative framework	It is recommended that Trinidad and Tobago take steps to include an effective date for the requirement to file CbC reports. It is recommended that Trinidad and Tobago publish the full content and format requirements of the CbC Report. It is recommended that Trinidad and Tobago take steps to ensure that local filing only occurs in the circumstances permitted under the minimum standard. It is recommended that Trinidad and Tobago clarify that the annual consolidated group revenue threshold calculation rule applies in line with the OECD guidance on currency fluctuations in respect of an MNE Group whose Ultimate Parent Entity is located in a jurisdiction other than Trinidad and Tobago.
Exchange of information framework	It is recommended that Trinidad and Tobago take steps to have qualifying competent authority agreements in effect with jurisdictions of the Inclusive Framework that meet the confidentiality, consistency and appropriate use conditions and with which Trinidad and Tobago has an international exchange of information agreement in effect that allows for the automatic exchange of tax information. It is recommended that Trinidad and Tobago take steps to implement the necessary processes or written procedures to ensure that the exchange of information is conducted in a manner consistent with the terms of reference relating to the exchange of information framework.
Appropriate use	It is recommended that Trinidad and Tobago take steps to ensure that the appropriate use condition is met ahead of the first exchanges of information.

The domestic legal and administrative framework

Trinidad and Tobago's 2018/2019 peer review report included a recommendation to take steps to implement legislation to impose a CbC reporting filing requirement. Trinidad and Tobago has since introduced such a filing requirement and this recommendation is removed.[1]

As Trinidad and Tobago's legislation does not include a specific effective date, a legislative filing requirement is therefore not yet in effect in Trinidad and Tobago. Trinidad and Tobago should take steps to include an effective date for the requirement to file CbC reports.

There are a number of areas where there are recommendations to improve the legislation.

Effective date

Trinidad and Tobago's legislation does not take effect until the proclamation of the legislation by the President of Trinidad and Tobago. It is recommended that Trinidad and Tobago take steps to include an effective date for the requirement to file CbC reports.

Contents of the Country-by-Country report

The information included in the legislation does not include all of the template of the Country-by-Country report and does not include any details of what should be included under each heading in the report. It is recommended that Trinidad and Tobago publish the full content and format requirements of the CbC Report.

The local filing provision

Trinidad and Tobago has a legislative requirement which is in effect despite Trinidad and Tobago not yet meeting all of the consistency, confidentiality and appropriate use conditions. It is therefore recommended that Trinidad and Tobago take steps to ensure that local filing only occurs in the circumstances permitted under the minimum standard.

Currency Fluctuations

Where an MNE Group draws up, or would draw up, its Consolidated Financial Statements in a currency other than that specified by Trinidad and Tobago, the reference to Trinidad and Tobago's threshold has the effect as if it were a reference to the equivalent in that currency at the average exchange rate for the accounting period. While this provision would not create an issue for MNE Groups whose Ultimate Parent Entity is a tax resident in Trinidad and Tobago, it may be incompatible with the guidance on currency fluctuations for MNE Groups whose Ultimate Parent Entity is located in another jurisdiction, if local filing requirements were applied in respect of a Constituent Entity (which is a Trinidad and Tobago tax resident) of an MNE Group which does not reach the threshold as determined in the jurisdiction of the Ultimate Parent Entity of such a Group.

It is recommended that Trinidad and Tobago clarify that the annual consolidated group revenue threshold calculation rule applies in line with the OECD guidance on currency fluctuations in respect of an MNE Group whose Ultimate Parent Entity is located in a jurisdiction other than Trinidad and Tobago.

The exchange of information framework

Trinidad and Tobago has no bilateral relationships in place for the exchange of CbC reports nor processes to ensure that the exchange of information is conducted in a manner consistent with the terms of reference relating to the exchange of information framework.

It is recommended that Trinidad and Tobago take steps to have qualifying competent authority agreements in effect with jurisdictions of the Inclusive Framework that meet the confidentiality, consistency and appropriate use conditions and with which Trinidad and Tobago has an international exchange of information agreement in effect that allows for the automatic exchange of tax information. This recommendation remains in place since the 2018/2019 peer review.

It is recommended that Trinidad and Tobago take steps to implement the necessary processes or written procedures to ensure that the exchange of information is conducted in a manner consistent with the terms of reference relating to the exchange of information framework. This recommendation remains in place since the 2018/2019 peer review.

Appropriate use of CbC reports

Trinidad and Tobago does not yet have controls in place to ensure the appropriate use of CbC reports.

It is recommended that Trinidad and Tobago take steps to ensure that the appropriate use condition is met ahead of the first exchanges of information. This recommendation remains in place since the 2018/2019 peer review.

Note

[1] https://www.ttparliament.org/wp-content/uploads/2023/11/a2024-02g.pdf

Tunisia

Overview of CbC reporting requirements

First reporting fiscal year: Commencing on or after 1 January 2020

Consolidated group revenue threshold: TND 1.636 billion

Filing deadline: 12 months following the end of the reporting fiscal year

Local filing required: Requirement suspended

Surrogate parent entity filing permitted: No

First review of the domestic legal framework: 2018/2019

Summary of recommendations

Area of implementation	Recommendations for improvement
Domestic legal and administrative framework	None.
Exchange of information framework	None.
Appropriate use	Not reviewed.

The domestic legal and administrative framework

Tunisia confirms that its rules have not changed and continue to be applied effectively. Tunisia continues to meet all terms of reference.

The exchange of information framework

Tunisia confirms that its rules have not changed and continue to be applied effectively. Tunisia continues to meet all terms of reference.

Appropriate use of CbC reports

Tunisia is a non-reciprocal jurisdiction and, as such, will not receive CbC reports submitted to tax authorities in other jurisdictions. It is therefore not necessary for this peer review evaluation to reach any conclusions with respect to Tunisia's compliance with the terms of reference on appropriate use.

Türkiye

Overview of CbC reporting requirements

First reporting fiscal year: Commencing on or after 1 January 2019

Consolidated group revenue threshold: EUR 750 million

Filing deadline: 12 months following the end of the reporting fiscal year

Local filing required: Yes

Surrogate parent entity filing permitted: Yes

First review of the domestic legal framework: 2019/2020

Summary of recommendations

Area of implementation	Recommendations for improvement
Domestic legal and administrative framework	None.
Exchange of information framework	None.
Appropriate use	None.

The domestic legal and administrative framework

Türkiye confirms that its rules have not changed and continue to be applied effectively. Türkiye continues to meet all terms of reference.

The exchange of information framework

Türkiye confirms that its rules have not changed and continue to be applied effectively. Türkiye continues to meet all terms of reference.

Appropriate use of CbC reports

Türkiye confirms that its rules have not changed and continue to be applied effectively. Türkiye continues to meet all terms of reference.

Turks and Caicos Islands

Overview of CbC reporting requirements

First reporting fiscal year: Commencing on or after 1 January 2020

Consolidated group revenue threshold: USD 850 million

Filing deadline: 12 months following the end of the reporting fiscal year

Local filing required: No

Surrogate parent entity filing permitted: No

First review of the domestic legal framework: 2018/2019

Summary of recommendations

Area of implementation	Recommendations for improvement
Domestic legal and administrative framework	None.
Exchange of information framework	None.
Appropriate use	Not reviewed.

The domestic legal and administrative framework

Turks and Caicos Islands confirms that its rules have not changed and continue to be applied effectively. Turks and Caicos Islands continues to meet all terms of reference.

The exchange of information framework

Turks and Caicos Islands confirms that its rules have not changed and continue to be applied effectively. Turks and Caicos Islands continues to meet all terms of reference.

Appropriate use of CbC reports

Turks and Caicos Islands is a non-reciprocal jurisdiction and, as such, will not receive CbC reports submitted to tax authorities in other jurisdictions, and will not apply local filing. It is therefore not necessary for this peer review evaluation to reach any conclusions with respect to compliance with the terms of reference on appropriate use.

Ukraine

Overview of CbC reporting requirements

First reporting fiscal year: Ending in the period from 1 January to 31 December 2022 for Ukrainian resident MNEs. (Beginning in the period from 1 January to 31 December of year when the MCAA will be activated for non-resident MNEs)

Consolidated group revenue threshold: EUR 750 million

Filing deadline: 12 months following the end of the reporting fiscal year

Local filing required: Requirement suspended

Surrogate parent entity filing permitted: Yes

First review of the domestic legal framework: 2020/2021

Summary of recommendations

Area of implementation	Recommendations for improvement
Domestic legal and administrative framework	None.
Exchange of information framework	None.
Appropriate use	None.

The domestic legal and administrative framework

Ukraine confirms its rules have not changed and continue to be applied effectively. Ukraine continues to meet all terms of reference.

The exchange of information framework

Ukraine's 2017/2018 peer review included a recommendation that Ukraine take steps to have qualifying competent authority agreements in effect with jurisdictions of the Inclusive Framework that meet the confidentiality, consistency and appropriate use conditions and with which Ukraine has an international exchange of information agreement in effect that allows for the automatic exchange of tax information. Ukraine has activated relationships under the Multilateral Competent Authority Agreement for the exchange of CbC reports and this recommendation is removed.

Ukraine has provided details of the written procedures in place to ensure that the exchange of information is conducted in a manner consistent with the terms of reference relating to the exchange of information framework.

Ukraine confirms that its rules have not changed and continue to be applied effectively.

Appropriate use of CbC reports

Ukraine confirms that its rules have not changed and continue to be applied effectively. Ukraine continues to meet all terms of reference.

United Arab Emirates

Overview of CbC reporting requirements

First reporting fiscal year: Commencing on or after 1 January 2019

Consolidated group revenue threshold: AED 3.15 billion

Filing deadline: 12 months following the end of the reporting fiscal year

Local filing required: No

Surrogate parent entity filing permitted: No

First review of the domestic legal framework: 2019/2020

Summary of recommendations

Area of implementation	Recommendations for improvement
Domestic legal and administrative framework	None.
Exchange of information framework	None.
Appropriate use	Not reviewed.

The domestic legal and administrative framework

UAE confirms that its rules have not changed and continue to be applied effectively. UAE continues to meet all terms of reference.

The exchange of information framework

UAE confirms that its rules have not changed and continue to be applied effectively. UAE continues to meet all terms of reference.

Appropriate use of CbC reports

UAE is a non-reciprocal jurisdiction and, as such, will not receive CbC reports submitted to tax authorities in other jurisdictions, and will not apply local filing. It is therefore not necessary for this peer review evaluation to reach any conclusions with respect to compliance with the terms of reference on appropriate use.

United Kingdom

Overview of CbC reporting requirements

First reporting fiscal year: Commencing on or after 1 January 2016

Consolidated group revenue threshold: EUR 750 million

Filing deadline: 12 months following the end of the reporting fiscal year

Local filing required: Yes

Surrogate parent entity filing permitted: Yes

First review of the domestic legal framework: 2017/2018

Summary of recommendations

Area of implementation	Recommendations for improvement
Domestic legal and administrative framework	None.
Exchange of information framework	None.
Appropriate use	None.

The domestic legal and administrative framework

The United Kingdom introduced a new power to make regulations which has replaced the power under which the regulations were originally laid, and which does not impact the operation of its rules for CbC reporting in practice.[1]

The United Kingdom has removed its CbC reporting notification requirement.[2]

The United Kingdom confirms that its rules have not changed and continue to be applied effectively. The United Kingdom continues to meet all terms of reference.[3]

The exchange of information framework

The United Kingdom confirms that its rules have not changed and continue to be applied effectively. The United Kingdom continues to meet all terms of reference.

Appropriate use of CbC reports

The United Kingdom confirms that its rules have not changed and continue to be applied effectively. The United Kingdom continues to meet all terms of reference.

Notes

[1] https://www.legislation.gov.uk/ukdsi/2023/9780348251128

[2] https://www.legislation.gov.uk/uksi/2023/752/contents/made

[3] The United Kingdom's 2017/2018 peer review included monitoring points with respect to the conditions under which local filing may be required (paragraph 8 (c) iv. b) and c) of the terms of reference). These monitoring points remain in place.

United States

Overview of CbC reporting requirements

First reporting fiscal year: Commencing on or after 30 June 2016, The United States also allowed MNE Groups to file a CbC report on a voluntary basis, for reporting fiscal years commencing between 1 January 2016 and 30 June 2016.

Consolidated group revenue threshold: USD 850 million

Filing deadline: with the annual income tax return

Local filing required: No

Surrogate parent entity filing permitted: Yes

First review of the domestic legal framework: 2017/2018

Summary of recommendations

Area of implementation	Recommendations for improvement
Domestic legal and administrative framework	It is recommended that the United States ensure that the definitions of "revenue" for the purposes of applying the threshold and for completing Table 1 are consistent with the definition in the Action 13 minimum standard, as further clarified by OECD guidance.
Exchange of information framework	It is recommended that the United States' competent authority should continue to work actively towards signing bilateral competent authority arrangements with jurisdictions of the Inclusive Framework that meet the confidentiality, consistency and appropriate use conditions, and with which the United States has an agreement in effect that allows for the automatic exchange of information.
Appropriate use	None.

The domestic legal and administrative framework

It is recommended that the United States ensure that the definitions of "revenue" for the purposes of applying the threshold and for completing Table 1 are consistent with the definition in the Action 13 minimum standard, as further clarified by OECD guidance. This recommendation remains in place since the 2017/2018 peer review.[1]

The exchange of information framework

The United States notified some late exchanges of CbC reports, due to a technical issue. This has now been fixed and so no recommendation has been made.

It is recommended that the United States' competent authority should continue to work actively towards signing bilateral competent authority arrangements with jurisdictions of the Inclusive Framework that meet the confidentiality, consistency and appropriate use conditions, and with which the United States has an agreement in effect that allows for the automatic exchange of information. This recommendation remains in place since the 2017/2018 peer review.

Appropriate use of CbC reports

The United States confirms that its rules have not changed and continue to be applied effectively. The United States continues to meet all terms of reference.

Note

[1] The United States operates a modified filing requirement for MNEs which qualify as state security contractors. In light of the United States' explanations and the limited number of MNE Groups that are likely to qualify for the specified national security contractor status, no recommendation is made, but use of modified reporting will be monitored. This monitoring point remains in place since the 2018/2019 peer review.

Uruguay

Overview of CbC reporting requirements

First reporting fiscal year: Commencing on or after 1 January 2017

Consolidated group revenue threshold: EUR 750 million

Filing deadline: 12 months following the end of the reporting fiscal year

Local filing required: Yes

Surrogate parent entity filing permitted: Yes

First review of the domestic legal framework: 2017/2018

Summary of recommendations

Area of implementation	Recommendations for improvement
Domestic legal and administrative framework	It is recommended that Uruguay amend the conditions for local filing or otherwise take steps to ensure that local filing can only be required in the circumstances contained in the terms of reference.
Exchange of information framework	None.
Appropriate use	None.

The domestic legal and administrative framework

It is recommended that Uruguay amend the conditions for local filing or otherwise take steps to ensure that local filing can only be required in the circumstances contained in the terms of reference. This recommendation remains in place since the 2017/2018 peer review.

The exchange of information framework

Uruguay confirms that its rules have not changed and continue to be applied effectively. Uruguay continues to meet all terms of reference.

Appropriate use of CbC reports

Uruguay confirms that its rules have not changed and continue to be applied effectively. Uruguay continues to meet all terms of reference.

Uzbekistan

Overview of CbC reporting requirements

Uzbekistan has not yet introduced a requirement for the filing of CbC reports, as required under the BEPS Action 13 (CbC reporting) minimum standard.

Summary of recommendations

Area of implementation	Recommendations for improvement
Domestic legal and administrative framework	It is recommended that Uzbekistan take steps to implement a domestic legal and administrative framework to impose and enforce CbC reporting requirements as soon as possible.
Exchange of information framework	It is recommended that Uzbekistan take steps to have qualifying competent authority agreements in effect with jurisdictions of the Inclusive Framework that meet the confidentiality, consistency and appropriate use conditions and with which Uzbekistan has an international exchange of information agreement in effect that allows for the automatic exchange of tax information. It is recommended that Uzbekistan take steps to implement the necessary processes or written procedures to ensure that the exchange of information is conducted in a manner consistent with the terms of reference relating to the exchange of information framework.
Appropriate use	It is recommended that Uzbekistan take steps to ensure that the appropriate use condition is met ahead of the first exchanges of information.

The domestic legal and administrative framework

Uzbekistan does not yet have legislation in place to implement the BEPS Action 13 minimum standard.

It is recommended that Uzbekistan take steps to implement a domestic legal and administrative framework to impose and enforce CbC reporting requirements as soon as possible.

The exchange of information framework

Uzbekistan has no bilateral relationships in place for the exchange of CbC reports nor processes to ensure that the exchange of information is conducted in a manner consistent with the terms of reference relating to the exchange of information framework.

It is recommended that Uzbekistan take steps to have qualifying competent authority agreements in effect with jurisdictions of the Inclusive Framework that meet the confidentiality, consistency and appropriate use conditions and with which Uzbekistan has an international exchange of information agreement in effect that allows for the automatic exchange of tax information.

It is recommended that Uzbekistan take steps to implement the necessary processes or written procedures to ensure that the exchange of information is conducted in a manner consistent with the terms of reference relating to the exchange of information framework.

Appropriate use of CbC reports

Uzbekistan does not yet have controls in place to ensure the appropriate use of CbC reports.

It is recommended that Uzbekistan take steps to ensure that the appropriate use condition is met ahead of the first exchanges of information.

Viet Nam

Overview of CbC reporting requirements

First reporting fiscal year: Commencing on or after 1 May 2017

Consolidated group revenue threshold: VND 18 trillion

Filing deadline: On demand

Local filing required: Yes

Surrogate parent entity filing permitted: Yes

First review of the domestic legal framework: 2018/2019

Summary of recommendations

Area of implementation	Recommendations for improvement
Domestic legal and administrative framework	It is recommended that Viet Nam amend its legislation or otherwise take steps to ensure that enforcement provisions relating to the effective implementation of CbC reporting filing requirements are provided for as soon as possible. It is recommended that Viet Nam take steps to ensure that local filing only occurs in the circumstances permitted under the minimum standard.
Exchange of information framework	It is recommended that Viet Nam take steps to have qualifying competent authority agreements in effect with jurisdictions of the Inclusive Framework which meet the confidentiality, consistency and appropriate use conditions and with which it has an international exchange of information agreement in effect that allows for the automatic exchange of tax information. It is recommended that Viet Nam take steps to implement processes or written procedures to ensure that the exchange of information is conducted in a manner consistent with the terms of reference relating to the exchange of information framework as soon as possible.
Appropriate use	It is recommended that Viet Nam take steps to ensure that the appropriate use condition is met ahead of the first exchanges of information.

The domestic legal and administrative framework

It is recommended that Viet Nam amend its legislation or otherwise take steps to ensure that enforcement provisions relating to effective implementation of filing requirement for CbC reporting are provided for as required by the terms of reference as soon as possible. This recommendation remains in place since the 2018/2019 peer review.

Viet Nam has a legislative requirement for local filing which is in effect despite Viet Nam not yet meeting all of the consistency, confidentiality and appropriate use conditions. It is therefore recommended that Viet Nam take steps to ensure that local filing only occurs in the circumstances permitted under the minimum standard[1]. This recommendation remains in place since the 2022/2023 peer review.

Viet Nam's 2022/2023 peer review recommended that Viet Nam clarify that the annual consolidated group revenue threshold calculation rule applies in line with the OECD guidance on currency fluctuations in respect of an MNE Group whose Ultimate Parent Entity is located in a jurisdiction other than Viet Nam. Viet Nam has clarified that under its legislation local filing requirements cannot be applied in respect of a

Constituent Entity (which is a Viet Nam tax resident) of an MNE Group which does not reach the threshold as determined in the jurisdiction of the Ultimate Parent Entity of such a Group, and the recommendation is removed.

The exchange of information framework

Viet Nam has no bilateral relationships in place for the exchange of CbC reports nor processes to ensure that the exchange of information is conducted in a manner consistent with the terms of reference relating to the exchange of information framework.

It is recommended that Viet Nam take steps to have qualifying competent authority agreements in effect with jurisdictions of the Inclusive Framework which meet the confidentiality, consistency and appropriate use conditions and with which it has an international exchange of information agreement in effect that allows for the automatic exchange of tax information. This recommendation remains in place since the 2018/2019 peer review.

It is recommended that Viet Nam take steps to implement processes or written procedures to ensure that the exchange of information is conducted in a manner consistent with the terms of reference relating to the exchange of information framework as soon as possible. This recommendation remains in place since the 2018/2019 peer review.

Appropriate use of CbC reports

Viet Nam does not yet have controls in place to ensure the appropriate use of CbC reports.

It is recommended that Viet Nam take steps to ensure that the appropriate use condition is met ahead of the first exchanges of information. This recommendation remains in place since the 2018/2019 peer review.

Note

[1] Viet Nam's 2021/2022 peer review included a monitoring point with respect to the conditions under which local filing may be required (paragraph 8 (c) iv. c) of the terms of reference). This monitoring points remain in place.

Zambia

Overview of CbC reporting requirements

First reporting fiscal year: Ending on 31 December 2021

Consolidated group revenue threshold: EUR 750 million (ZMW 4.795 billion for Zambian resident MNE Groups)

Filing deadline: 12 months following the end of the reporting fiscal year

Local filing required: Yes

Surrogate parent entity filing permitted: Yes

First review of domestic legal framework: 2021/2022

Summary of recommendations

Area of implementation	Recommendations for improvement
Domestic legal and administrative framework	It is recommended that Zambia take steps to ensure that local filing only occurs in the circumstances permitted under the minimum standard. It is recommended that Zambia clarify that the annual consolidated group revenue threshold calculation rule applies in line with the OECD guidance on currency fluctuations in respect of an MNE Group whose Ultimate Parent Entity is located in a jurisdiction other than Zambia. It is recommended that Zambia publish the full content and format requirements of the CbC Report.
Exchange of information framework	It is recommended that Zambia take steps to have qualifying competent authority agreements in effect with jurisdictions of the Inclusive Framework that meet the confidentiality, consistency and appropriate use conditions and with which Zambia has an international exchange of information agreement in effect that allows for the automatic exchange of tax information. It is recommended that Zambia take steps to implement the necessary processes or written procedures to ensure that the exchange of information is conducted in a manner consistent with the terms of reference relating to the exchange of information framework.
Appropriate use	It is recommended that Zambia take steps to ensure that the appropriate use condition is met ahead of the first exchanges of information.

The domestic legal and administrative framework

Zambia's 2021/2022 peer review included a recommendation that Zambia amend the definition of MNE Group or otherwise clarify the definition to be in line with the standard. Zambia has amended the definition and this recommendation is therefore removed.

Zambia's 2021/2022 peer review included a recommendation that Zambia amend the definition of Ultimate Parent Entity or otherwise clarify the definition to be in line with the standard. Zambia has amended the definition and this recommendation is therefore removed.

Zambia's 2021/2022 peer review included a recommendation that Zambia amend the definition of MNE groups to specify that it does include excluded MNE groups, or to otherwise specify a threshold requirement for local filing. Zambia has amended the definition and this recommendation is therefore removed.

Zambia's 2021/2022 peer review included a recommendation that Zambia amend the definition of surrogate filing or otherwise clarify the definition to be in line with the standard. Zambia has amended the definition and this recommendation is therefore removed.

Zambia has a legislative requirement for local filing which is in line with the standard but which is in effect despite Zambia not yet meeting all of the consistency, confidentiality and appropriate use conditions. It is therefore recommended that Zambia take steps to ensure that local filing only occurs in the circumstances permitted under the minimum standard. This recommendation remains in place since the 2021/2022 peer review.

It is recommended that Zambia clarify that the annual consolidated group revenue threshold calculation rule applies in line with the OECD guidance on currency fluctuations in respect of an MNE Group whose Ultimate Parent Entity is located in a jurisdiction other than Zambia. This recommendation remains in place since the 2021/2022 peer review.

It is recommended that Zambia publish the full content and format requirements of the CbC Report. This recommendation remains in place since the 2021/2022 peer review.

The exchange of information framework

Zambia has no bilateral relationships in place for the exchange of CbC reports nor processes to ensure that the exchange of information is conducted in a manner consistent with the terms of reference relating to the exchange of information framework.

It is recommended that Zambia take steps to have qualifying competent authority agreements in effect with jurisdictions of the Inclusive Framework that meet the confidentiality, consistency and appropriate use conditions and with which Zambia has an international exchange of information agreement in effect that allows for the automatic exchange of tax information. This recommendation remains in place since the 2018/2019 peer review.

It is recommended that Zambia take steps to implement the necessary processes or written procedures to ensure that the exchange of information is conducted in a manner consistent with the terms of reference relating to the exchange of information framework. This recommendation remains in place since the 2018/2019 peer review.

Appropriate use of CbC reports

Zambia does not yet have controls in place to ensure the appropriate use of CbC reports.

It is recommended that Zambia take steps to ensure that the appropriate use condition is met ahead of the first exchanges of information. This recommendation remains in place since the 2018/2019 peer review.

www.ingramcontent.com/pod-product-compliance
Lightning Source LLC
Chambersburg PA
CBHW061207240926
51846CB00006B/1138